Richard Marian Ogorkiewicz
1926 - 2019

Acknowledgements

Before his death in November of last year my husband Professor Richard Ogorkiewicz had finished writing his autobiography but, he had neither editor or publisher. It is thanks to the unstinting labours of his friends and colleagues that this book is now seeing the light of day.

First and foremost thanks must go to Rupert Pengelley who took charge of Dick's manuscript and numerous boxes of uncatalogued photographs. Throughout the long months of lockdown Rupert devoted countless hours to editing Dick's manuscript and meticulously researching, sourcing and providing the captions for the many photos that enhance the book.

I should also like to thank Reece Dickinson who, with his artistic eye and presentational and design skills has done a brilliant job with the layout. Reece's flexibility and willingness to compromise were much appreciated.

My thanks are also due to David Willey, Curator of The Tank Museum who was determined to see Dick's book in print and who has been instrumental in getting the book published.

Jocelyn Ogorkiewicz   July 2020

Observer of Cold War tank development
Richard Ogorkiewicz

Contents

Introduction

This book is the outcome of a life-long interest in the development of tanks and other armoured vehicles. Even as a youngster I became interested in them, largely as a result of the successes of the German armoured forces in the early stages of the Second World War, in Poland in 1939 and in France in 1940. These affected me personally as, indirectly, they made me a refugee in Britain. Then, while pursuing engineering studies at university in London, I began to study the history and the characteristics of tanks and that of other armoured vehicles and from the basis of my studies I began to write about them for British, US and other military journals. In fact, in the 1950s and early 1960s I may have written more articles on tanks and armoured forces than anyone else did in the Western World at the time.

The articles and the publication of the first of my books led to invitations to lecture and to advise on tanks and their technology, not only in Britain but also in the United States, which provided opportunities to examine, at first hand, tanks developed in the two countries. I also developed contacts in Western Europe, which provided me with an insight into developments there and led to further advisory activities as well as more invitations to lecture.

As I became more widely known through my articles, books and lectures, I received invitations to lecture and to advise farther afield. This meant that in addition to all my activities in the United States and in Europe, I was invited to visit Israel and later to advise in another Middle Eastern country, namely Turkey. In the Far East I was invited to lecture in China, Japan and Singapore and saw the tanks developed in each of them, as well as lecturing and participating in tank development in South Korea. In the Southern Hemisphere I lectured and advised in Brazil, South Africa and Australia and again was able to study the armoured vehicles developed in them. Thus, during the period of the Cold War (1947-1991) and the decade which followed it, my activities took me to all five Continents.

My activities around the globe involved, in essence, disseminating knowledge about the characteristics and capabilities of tanks and other armoured vehicles by lecturing and writing on them. At the same time I was also able to study many of them at first hand and to contribute to their further development by advising thereon. In consequence, I acquired a broadly based view of tanks and this confirmed my opinion of their fundamental effectiveness as mobile, protected weapon platforms and, as such, as an effective component of the ground forces.

Chapter 1
Personal background

I never thought in my youth that much of my adult life would be connected with tanks, even though I was born and brought up in a military environment. However tanks did not feature in it at the time and I only became aware of them later, as I grew up.

My military environment was provided by my father who was an artillery officer in the Polish Army. Although still relatively young when I was born, he had already acquired considerable military experience starting in 1916 when, just before his 18th birthday, he was called up for service in the Imperial German Army, having been born in what was at the time the German ruled part of Poland. He was then assigned to a field artillery regiment of the Imperial German Army in which he served for the rest of the First World War on different sectors of the Western Front, including the Somme, during which he was wounded and was awarded the Iron Cross. At the Front he reached the rank of an officer candidate but was not promoted because his mother tongue was not German.

When the Imperial German Army collapsed in 1918, he made his way back to his home town and joined local defence volunteers who were fighting off attempts to re-impose German rule on the newly liberated Western Poland. He then joined as a lieutenant one of the artillery regiments of the newly created Polish Army and fought in all of its campaigns of 1919 and 1920, from the relief of Lwow, the most important city in Eastern Poland which was besieged by Ukrainian forces, and the brief capture by Polish forces of Kiew (the capital of the Ukraine), to the battle of Warsaw in which the invading Soviet Army was finally routed.

After the war my father's regiment, which became the 15th Field Artillery of the Polish Army and was equipped with horse-drawn 75 mm guns, was stationed in Bydgoszcz, a major town in Western Poland where it was originally raised. While serving in it he met and married my mother, who was a nurse in a local private clinic, and it was in Bydgoszcz that I was born in 1926.

1934 identity-card photograph of RMO's father Marian A. Ogorkiewicz, who was born in 1898 and died in 1963. He is wearing the uniform of a staff lieutenant colonel from the Polish Army's 15th Field Artillery Regiment. Note his Iron Cross, which he had won on the Western Front during previous First World War service in the ranks of the Imperial German Army's artillery arm.

The Ogorkiewicz family about town: a young RMO steps out between his mother Valdyna and his father Marian.

6

Christmas in Warsaw - RMO aged about 10 with his new model army, gaining an early insight into the merit of having the maximum of battlefield fire support on your own side

A more mature RMO on a return visit to his birthplace Bydgoszcz in the 1990s. He had always remembered the statue of 'the little angel' from the earliest days of his childhood, and was delighted to find it was still there.

Until 1933 my parents and I lived most of the time in Bydgoszcz, except for a year spent in Tarnopol in what was then eastern Poland when my father was assigned to the headquarters of an infantry division located there. One of the peculiarities of living in Tarnopol that I recall was a large number of holidays due to its mixed Polish, Ukrainian and Jewish population, each part of which observed its holidays at different times of the year, resulting in their large number in total. By then my father had graduated from the Staff College and was promoted a major and then a lieutenant colonel. He was then appointed to the General Staff of the Polish Army which was in Warsaw, so we moved there. We settled in a northern suburb called Zoliborz, a corruption of the French Joli Bord, or "Pretty Bank", which was bestowed on it because of its attractive location on the banks of the Vistula river by Piarist monks who settled in the area in the 18th century. Much more recently it has been described as the district of the Warsaw intellectuals!

While he was serving on the General Staff my father was responsible for most of the time for monitoring the military situation on the border of what was then East Prussia, including the garrison at Westerplatte at the mouth of the Vistula river where the first shots of the Second World War were later fired. But for a year or so he was assigned to the position of the second-in-command of a medium artillery regiment stationed at Modlin, a large old fortress north of Warsaw built in the 19th century by the Russians who were then occupying that part of Poland. As Modlin was not far from Warsaw we did not move house but I visited my father's regiment to see the equipment it had. In Warsaw I went to a small private "military family" school located a short walk from where we lived. The school was housed in an attractive, purpose-built building which had just been completed and which is still used by a school, having survived, intact, the ravages of the Second World War and is now regarded a part of the Polish cultural heritage. The most important event in its history was the disastrous Warsaw Uprising of 1944. This followed an ill-considered decision by the Polish Underground, called the Home Army, to come out into the open and fight the German occupying forces. However, the uprising was crushed and resulted in the wholesale destruction of the centre of Warsaw, including its historic Old Town, as well as misery for thousands of its inhabitants.

Well before this happened, I spent a couple of summer holidays with my parents at a resort on the Baltic coast and then at my uncle's small estate near Koscierzyna, a town in what was called the " Polish Corridor", the territory between East Prussia and Germany, where I enjoyed rural life.

In Warsaw I was a keen boy scout and marched as such in 1938 in the Independence Day parade on November 11, which celebrated Poland regaining its independence in 1918. I also took part in various other scout activities which included a week under canvas at a camp in the mountains in South East Poland in July 1939, little more than a month before the outbreak of the Second World War.

At one of the military parades in Warsaw a year or two before the war I saw tanks for the first time. I learnt later that they were designated 7TP and were a Polish development of the "Six-Ton" tank designed in Britain by Vickers-Armstrongs and produced for a number of countries, although it was not adopted by the British Army. 7TP came to weigh almost 10 tonnes and had a turret designed in Sweden by Bofors as well as being armed with a Bofors 37mm anti-tank gun, which made it comparable in this respect with other contemporary light/medium tanks. However, the Polish Army had only about 100 tanks of its type when the war broke out.

Polish Army 7TP tanks pass in review.

Second World War

By the time the war broke out I had completed my primary education and, having successfully passed the entrance exams into a well known local school, I was about to start my secondary education. Instead, as the war began to loom, I served as a boy scout at the local railway station distributing food to soldiers on passing troop-trains.

I recall little of interest happening during the first few days of the war, except for watching an aerial fight one day between some of the gull-winged fighter planes of the Polish Air Force and German bombers heading for Warsaw. As the Polish military situation deteriorated, the General Staff authorities organised an evacuation train for any military families that might wish to leave Warsaw and my mother and I decided to take advantage of this, leaving Warsaw on 5 September 1939. The train took us east, to a small town close to the border with the Soviet Union, and was machine gunned en route by a marauding German aircraft but without suffering serious damage. We stayed in that town for only a couple of days which was extremely fortunate as it avoided us being there when, ten days later, Soviet troops moved in. The train was re-directed south, to a small holiday town called Zaleszczyki on the Dniestr river which formed the border with Romania. The town had the reputation of being the warmest place in Poland and I enjoyed staying in it, one of its attractions being the walnuts growing on its trees.

Then, a week after our arrival, on 17 September, came the news that Soviet forces had invaded Poland. Fortunately, the evacuation train was still standing at the Zaleszczyki station where someone had had the foresight to fire the boiler of the locomotive so that the train was ready to move. We re-boarded it and it took us as well as others across the Dniestr river, into Romania, by a bridge which some German aircraft had tried to bomb. Had we stayed on the Polish side of the river we would have been arrested in all probability by the NKVD, the dreaded Soviet secret police, as members of the "Polish intelligentsia" which they persecuted, and ended in a forced labour camp or gulag.

We did not know at the time that my father was in the same part of the country, to which the General Staff retreated as the German forces advanced headed by their Panzer formations, and also narrowly escaped being captured by the invading Soviet troops. This happened as a result of being ordered on the day of the invasion to drive out in a staff car to find out what was happening on the Polish-Soviet border. On the way there he suddenly came up against a column of tanks advancing from the direction of the border and recognised them to be Soviet tanks. Their intentions were not clear but, having fought Soviet troops twenty years earlier, my father decided not to take

any chances and ordered the driver of his car to turn round and drive back as fast as he could before the Soviet tankers reacted in any way. Had he not done so he would have been taken prisoner and probably murdered later by the Soviet secret police in the infamous Katyn Forest, like thousands of other Polish Army officers captured by the Soviet Army. One of them was my favourite uncle, at whose estate in Western Poland I spent summer holidays. He was a reserve officer in the Polish Army and as such was taken prisoner by the Soviet forces, only to be executed in the Katyn Forest massacre in 1940.

The train aboard which my mother and I crossed into Romania was shunted for about a week around the Romanian railway system and eventually brought us to Călimănești, a very pleasant mountain resort in the centre of the country which was vacant at the time as we arrived out of season. The Romanians were generally sympathetic towards Poland but had to appear to be neutral to Germany and the Soviet Union, so Călimănești was designated an "internment camp" for Polish military and their families.

People with whom we came into contact in Călimănești and later in the neighbouring town of Vâlcea were mainly local peasants who were generally friendly and cheerful, in spite of their poverty. How poor they were was shown by their footwear which consisted of sections of car tyres cut to form sandals of sorts and which they wore even at the height of the winter, when the snow was more than a foot deep. Nevertheless, they were generally honest which is more than could be said of the higher strata of Romanian society: even a policeman could be bribed to allow jumping an office queue which he might have been guarding. At the top of what was generally perceived to be a pyramid of corruption stood the king, Carol II who was in effect a dictator, and his widely known mistress, Magda Lupescu.

The staple item of peasant food was a vegetable soup called ciorba which could be very palatable. To avoid stomach upsets, particularly during the train journey, we refrained as far as possible from drinking water and resorted instead to the local wine which was weak but pleasant. In addition to ciorba and the wine, I also came to enjoy listening to the simple, peasant music, played mainly on fiddles, for which I have retained a liking. I also began to speak Romanian, even after only three months, which was relatively easy to do as it contained an admixture of Latin, French and Slav words.

My father had also crossed into Romania on the day of the Soviet invasion, as did the rest of the Polish General Staff. However, he found himself on his own in Zaleszczyki and as the Soviet patrols approached he crossed into Romania, on foot, with a few of the Polish soldiers who were still in the town, over the same railway bridge as that over which the evacuation train had rolled earlier in the day. Shortly after crossing into Romania my father became very seriously ill but luckily fell into the hands of a very kind doctor who was a medical officer in the Granicerii, the Romanian Frontier Guards, and who nursed him back to health. For a time he was kept on a very strict diet which consisted only of scraped apples!

After a while my father was well enough to be transferred from Cernauti, where he was recovering, to another of the so-called internment camps in a different locality from the one in which my mother and I were in. However, in November 1939 we were reunited and at the end of January travelled to Bucharest where the Polish consulate was still functioning to obtain passports with false names which would enable us to leave Romania where my father was supposed to remain interned. From Romania we travelled, by train, through Yugoslavia and Italy, which was still neutral at the time, to France. We arrived at the border town of Modane on 5 February 1940, where we met a Polish Army liaison officer. We then travelled on to Paris where father reported to the headquarters of the Polish forces which were being re-created in France and was assigned to them. The headquarters were located in Hotel Regina, a grand hotel across the Rue de Rivoli from the Louvre museum, which was taken over by the French authorities for military purposes at the beginning of the war. In front of the hotel stands a statue of Joan of Arc which was gilded during the German occupation of France to show that she also fought against the English!

As my father's duties kept him in Paris we settled there and I went to a Franco-Polish school on the Left Bank. The following three months passed pleasantly and peacefully, in spite of France being at war, the calm being encouraged by numerous posters showing, among others, how much greater was the combined territory of the French and British empires compared with that of Germany. Some of the museums and galleries remained open and I took advantage of this to visit some of them, including the military museum at Les Invalides. At the same time, prompted by the successes of the German tank forces in Poland the previous year, I began to study what information there was about tanks in French journals and magazines.

The calm of what came to be called the "Phoney War" was shattered on 10 May 1940 when the German forces launched their offensive against France and the Low Countries. As they advanced Polish military families we knew began to leave Paris and we followed their example on 27 May by going, by train, to Arcachon, a very pleasant seaside town south of Bordeaux. We stayed there until 21 June when we were given a lift in a truck to Saint Jean de Luz, a small port close to the border with Spain.

There, on the following day, on which France surrendered to Germany, we embarked on MS *Batory* which had come to evacuate some Polish Army troops to Britain.

A pre-war photograph of the Polish liner MS *Batory*, on which RMO and his mother made their escape from St Jean de Luz in 1940.

MS *Batory* was an Italian-built Polish liner of 14,000 tons which before the war sailed regularly between Gdynia in Poland and New York. It was too big to enter the small harbour of Saint Jean de Luz and in the absence of adequate port facilities the embarkation had to be carried out using the ship's lifeboats. My mother and I embarked on the last of them, in the dead of night and had to leave what little luggage we still had on the quayside. In consequence, when we arrived in Plymouth three days later we had nothing but the clothes on our backs.

Nevertheless, we were lucky to reach Britain on MS *Batory* because, unknown to us at the time, its merchant seamen crew became fearful of rumours of U-boats operating in the Bay of Biscay and of German bombers flying over it, and had earlier refused to sail out of Plymouth unless their ship was escorted by a warship. This demand could not be met and the mutiny was quickly brought to an end by a detachment of armed Polish Navy sailors who boarded the ship and arrested the principal mutineers, after which the ship sailed out of Plymouth to Saint Jean de Luz, as ordered. I clearly recall armed sailors being on the ship at the time but did not learn why they were there until many years later, as the mutiny was hushed up.

Having delivered us to Plymouth, MS *Batory* continued to serve as a troopship for the rest of the Second World War, taking part in several major landing operations. After the war it reverted for a number of years to the role of a passenger liner. Its sister ship, MS *Pilsudski*, was far less fortunate. To escape falling into German hands, it sailed from Poland to Britain shortly before the outbreak of the war but, within three months of it, hit mines laid secretly by a German warship off the British east coast and sank.

After we landed in Plymouth on 25 June 1940 we were taken with other refugees by train to London, under armed escort, presumably because of rumours which were widespread at the time that the refugees were infiltrated by German spies. Having been cleared we, like others, were assigned to British families willing to accommodate refugees. My mother and I were very lucky to be adopted by Lady Williamson-Noble who put us up in a mews cottage vacated by her driver who was away on national service. The cottage was close to Harley Street where she lived with her husband who was one of Britain's leading eye surgeons and practised there. She was most kind to us and even apologised for not being able to offer us better accommodation, as well as inviting us for a weekend at the house she had on edge of the world famous Wentworth Golf Club.

In the wake of the German offensive in France my father was transferred with others from Paris to Coetquidan in Brittany, where there was a large camp built during the First World War for American troops. This was taken over at the beginning of the Second World War by the Polish Army when it was being re-created in France. From there he managed, somehow, to make his way to La Rochelle where he found himself in charge of the evacuation of some Polish troops and from which he was the last to leave, on the Canadian destroyer HMCS *Restigouche*. After arriving in Britain he was directed to London, where we found him through the Red Cross. He was then posted to Scotland to join Polish troops who had managed to escape from France and were being deployed to guard the East Coast, while my mother and I remained in London where we bought some clothes and began to learn English - of which we did not speak a word when we arrived!

The Canadian destroyer HMCS *Restigouche* which rescued RMO's father from La Rochelle, as part of Operation Aerial.

The first two months passed peacefully and pleasantly: the shops were still well stocked and food rationing was not by any means onerous. But then the German aerial bombing campaign began. At first we took little notice of it, beyond observing clouds of black smoke arising from the area of London's docks. As bombs began to fall on the centre of London we followed official advice to go at night to a designated air-raid shelter, although this proved to be little more than the basement of a large house in the vicinity. The house escaped a direct hit, although some bombs fell very close to it and I remember some people who were less fortunate than we were being brought into the shelter all covered with dust from a nearby bomb explosion. The house also avoided being hit by incendiary bombs, unlike the large John Lewis department store in nearby Oxford Street, in Central London, the whole of which we saw ablaze as we emerged one morning from the shelter after the "all clear" siren was sounded.

As there was no reason for us to stay in London, particularly as my father was in Scotland, we decided to leave for Edinburgh, which we did on 20 September 1940. After settling there and spending some more time learning English, I was recommended by a doctor, a Polish Army friend of my father's, to one of the masters at George Heriot's School. On the latter's advice I applied for admission and after being interviewed was accepted by the School in 1941.

The imposing approach to George Heriot's School off Lauriston Place in the shadow of Edinburgh Castle.

George Heriot's School is an independent school founded in 1628 by a jeweller to King James VI of Scotland and is overlooked by Edinburgh Castle, its main purpose-built building being an outstanding example of renaissance architecture. In addition to its impressive setting, I found the School to be very friendly and was fully accepted by my schoolmates in spite of being obviously a recently arrived foreigner. The very friendly reception accorded to me contrasted with the animosity some of the boys showed at times towards the English, or 'Sassenachs' as they were

colloquially called. An extreme example of this was provided by a meeting of the School debating society, soon after the 1942 victory of the British Army at the battle of El Alamein in which the Scottish 51st Highland Division played a very prominent part. This prompted one of the senior boys to claim that the English advanced to victory over the bodies of dead Scots!

I happily took part in various School activities which included joining the Junior Training Corps. This involved wearing, on appropriate occasions, a kilt as part of its uniform which I was very proud to do. At School I also acquired an affection for the sound of bagpipes. Although the School had a pipe band I did not join it but I loved marching behind it and even now, many years later, I am thrilled by the sound of bagpipes. Without realizing it, I also acquired a strong Scottish accent, as a result of which, when I went later to university in London, my English fellow-students used to call me "Jock", i.e. Scotsman!

The doctor who directed me to George Heriot's School was a senior surgeon in the Polish Army and was at the time running an impromptu course at Edinburgh University for Polish Army medical officer cadets. One of the problems he had was a shortage of suitable blackboard diagrams and to help I drew several for him, on large sheets of brown paper! He, in turn, performed a minor operation on one of my feet which had become infected during the course of our peregrinations. This took place in the British Army military hospital to which he was attached, located at the time at Edinburgh Castle.

After a time I lost my Scottish accent but I kept in touch with the School and after the war when the London Heriot Club was revived I joined it with other Former Pupils, or FPs, living in the London area. For a time I even acted as honorary assistant secretary of the Club.

While I was still at school in Edinburgh my father was serving in the headquarters of the Polish forces in Scotland, which were located at Bridge of Earn in Fife where I visited him a few times. But the forces were then reorganized into an airborne brigade and an armoured division and my father was assigned to the latter.

The armoured division was moved from Scotland to the neighbourhood of Scarborough, in Yorkshire, where there was enough land for tanks to manoeuvre and I visited my father there once when I was able to see some of the tanks with which the division was equipped. But my father was then suddenly transferred to the headquarters of the Polish forces in exile, which were located in London at the Rubens Hotel that had been taken over for military purposes and was very close to Buckingham Palace.

RMO at the door to the Imperial College of Science and Technology in London, into which he was accepted at the age of 17.

I had by that time completed my secondary education and I followed my father back to London. I was too young for military service, which made it possible for me to start studying engineering that I wanted to pursue. I was advised by some scientist friends of my father to go to the Imperial College of Science and Technology, part of the University of London, and I applied for admission, being accepted in 1943 to study mechanical engineering. After successfully completing the first year of studies, my call up for military service was deferred on the grounds that engineering was a "reserved occupation". So I was left to continue my studies and after two more years I graduated with the degree of Batchelor of Science in Engineering in 1946. By then the war was over and I was no longer wanted for service in the Polish forces in Britain which were being disbanded.

The intervening years passed uneventfully except for the German V-1 Flying Bombs, or "Doodlebugs" as they were commonly called, which began to fall on London in June 1944 when Allied forces were landing in Normandy, one of the bombs exploding close to where I lived. During the first summer vacation I worked as trainee mechanic in a small engineering company in Watford, under a training scheme operated by Imperial College to foster practical engineering experience. In the second summer vacation I also worked as a trainee mechanic but in another small engineering company.

Although I already had a degree I decided to stay at Imperial College on a post graduate studentship, partly because of the uncertain political situation created by the Foreign Office which was urging Poles in Britain to return to Poland in spite of it being under Soviet occupation. I had no intention of leaving Britain and as soon as possible applied for British citizenship, which I was granted in 1949. My father also remained in Britain, having been deprived of Polish nationality by the Communist government in power in Warsaw, together with General Anders, the commander-in-chief of the Polish forces in exile, and other senior Polish Army officers.

During the first postgraduate year I worked for a short time as a graduate trainee in the research department of Leyland Motors in Lancashire, who were then in the forefront of the development of truck and bus diesel engines and who provided me with a valuable insight therein. A year later I also spent some time as an engineering trainee in Coventry with Armstrong Siddeley Motors, who were developing one of the world's first turboprop engines to be built, called Mamba.

I remained at Imperial College for three years as an assistant lecturer, teaching and doing research into the aerodynamics of turbine blades, for which I was awarded eventually the degree of Master of Science in Engineering. During this period, in 1950, I made the first of my many visits to the United States. As contemporary regulations did not allow taking out of Britain more than £5 in cash, the visit was only possible because relatives in New York very generously promised to look after me once I landed in the United States. So I bought an economy-class ticket to sail on SS *Washington*, which had not fully recovered from being a troopship during the war. In fact, it was still painted grey and I had to share a cabin with five young Americans some of who, very generously, bought me a drink or two during the journey knowing how little money I was allowed to have!

SS *Washington*, still decked out as the troopship USS *Vernon*, conveyed RMO on his first visit to the United States in 1950.

After I landed in New York my relatives took me touring, by car, to Niagara Falls and as far as Quebec in Canada and then back through the New England states to New York. I then travelled by train on my own from Grand Central Station in New York to Chicago, Illinois, in a train called "Wolverine" which was air-conditioned and very different in several other respects from the trains run at the time in Britain. My reason for going to Chicago was to visit Colonel Robert J. Icks with whom I had established contact four years earlier after the publication of his book "Tanks and armored vehicles" and with whom I was going to correspond for many years. While I was staying with him he very kindly allowed me to look through his considerable collection of documents about the history of tanks. I then went on to Detroit where, thanks to introductions from Bob Icks, I was able to visit on successive days the three major US car companies, General Motors, Ford and Chrysler, who between them were at the time producing 5 million cars per year, or about 80 per cent of the world's total car production. Then, trying a different form of US transportation, I went by Greyhound coach to visit Colonel G.B. Jarrett, who was director of the Ordnance Museum at the Aberdeen Proving Ground in Maryland, to see the historical collection of tanks there. I then continued to Washington DC where I spent a couple of days sight-seeing, during which I managed to visit the National Gallery, Smithsonian Institute, and Mount Vernon, Virginia, the home of George Washington. From Washington I went back to New York to spend a week with relatives. After a total of more than two months, I sailed back to Britain on SS *Veendam*, a Dutch ship which took ten days to sail from New York to Southampton but this time I had a cabin to myself.

Back at Imperial College I decided that I should acquire some industrial engineering experience. I would have liked to acquire it in the tank industry and applied for a job with the Ministry of Supply which was controlling it, but my application was turned down because I was not British born. I did better in 1952 when I applied for a job with the Engineering Division of the Ford Motor Company at Dagenham in Essex. Because my research at Imperial College was related to the aerodynamics of turbine blades, I was assigned to work on gas turbines which were expected to be the car engines of the future. In consequence, soon after reporting for work, I was sent to attend a course at the School of Gas Turbine Technology at Farnborough, which was one of the centres of British gas turbine development and which enabled me to acquire more knowledge about it. After this I spent several dreary days at the Patent Office examining, on behalf of the Engineering Division of Fords, gas turbine patents. However, all this came to nothing as an edict came from Dearborn that any Ford Motor Company work on car gas-turbine engines would be concentrated in the United States: this left me high and dry!

After a short hiatus I was put on a management trainee course which involved working for short periods of time in different parts of the company, including the only blast furnace in the South of England. All this provided a valuable insight into the working of a modern, well-integrated industrial organization. The course also happened to coincide with London's Great Smog of 1952, when even the Ford Motor Company was obliged to cease operations in the middle of an afternoon as poisonous cyanide fumes from the heat-treatment baths of metal components began to mix with the fog. The visibility was reduced to a few feet and it was quite an eerie experience to walk out of the factory in the company of hundreds of men in almost complete silence, as all sounds were muffled by the fog.

The Company was not sure what to do with me when the prospects of work on gas turbines fizzled out, partly because I was the first engineering graduate it had employed.

Eventually I became a diesel development engineer which provided me with more experience of diesel engines. This stood me in good stead later, when I became involved in discussions about the use of different types of engines in tanks. During the time that I was concerned at Fords with engines, I was sent to Paris to report on a novel valveless "Toric" engine which was being offered by its French inventor. In consequence I flew - for the first time - to Paris and spent a day there discussing the "Toric" engine with its inventor. On my return I wrote a long report, with diagram of the engine, the gist of which was that the "Toric" engine was interesting mechanically but was not proven. Thus it would not have been appropriate for the Ford Motor Company in Britain, which was geared to the production of well-established products rather than development of new ones, to take it up.

While working at Fords I also acquired my first car, a 1.6 litre Consul, taking advantage of a Company scheme which enabled employees to buy its cars at a discount and I actually drove my car off the end of the final assembly line.However, after a time I decided to move on and took up the offer of a job in the engineering department of another car company, Humber Ltd, which was located in Coventry and was part of the Rootes Group of car and truck companies. There I became an assistant to the chief engineering executive. I found my new employers friendly but I was not impressed with the company from the engineering point of view, or with the cars it produced, and it failed to provide me with any further worthwhile experience - except for the opportunity to test-drive different makes of cars that I could borrow from the Research Department, which had acquired them to study and compare with Humber's own cars.

After two years of working in Coventry, the head of the mechanical engineering department at Imperial College, where I previously studied and worked, offered me a job as a lecturer: I decided to take it up, particularly as contemporary university salaries were not very different from pay in the automobile industry.

A 1952 1.6-litre Ford Consul, such as that RMO was able to buy at advantageous rates from his first employer. At that time Ford had plans to adapt gas-turbine engines to cars.

Dealing with plastics

After a couple of years of conventional lecturing I was asked to lead studies of the mechanical properties of plastics, which were coming into greater use as engineering materials. In consequence I was asked to start a new kind of post-graduate course on plastics and to set up a small plastics-testing laboratory. This led me, among others, to devise a novel type of double-pendulum machine for impact-testing plastics films, five replicas of which were subsequently made for industrial laboratories in Britain and the United States.

I also pursued research into the mechanical properties of plastics, which ultimately led me to the publication of about 50 research papers and articles, as well as presentations at conferences in Britain, Italy and Belgium and also in the United States. One of the US conferences was held in 1968 in New York by the Society of Plastics Engineers to commemorate the centenary of the production of the first plastics article, which was made to replace the traditional ivory billiards ball: the original plastics balls were made of nitrocellulose and went off occasionally with a bang. This led to a letter from a saloon owner in Colorado, quoted at the Conference, complaining that when this happened all his customers drew their guns!

My activities also brought me into contact with the Plastics Division of Imperial Chemical Industries, or ICI, which was trying to promote a more rational use of plastics in engineering and which appointed me a consultant to it. As such I edited and contributed to two collective works produced by the Plastics Division entitled "Engineering properties of thermoplastics" and "Thermoplastics: properties and design" which were published, respectively, in 1970 and 1974 by John Wiley.

My work with ICI involved frequent visits to Welwyn Garden City where its Plastics Division was located, but its relatively short distance from Imperial College in London, when road traffic congestion had not yet become a problem, made visits by car easy.

In 1963 I also became a member of the Plastics Institute, in which I was involved in the formation of committees aimed at advancing rational design in plastics. In recognition of my activities I was made a Fellow of the Institute in 1973. During the same period I also served on the plastics and composite materials committees of the Ministry of Aviation and of the Ministry of Technology until they were dissolved and then on the Plastics Design Data Committee of the British Standards Institution.

But, for all this, I slowly came to the conclusion that my involvement with plastics was not going to lead me to any advancement at Imperial College and in 1985 I resigned from the latter to concentrate on my consulting and other activities connected with armoured vehicles which I pursued over the years concurrently with my academic work.

The ever-elegant and indomitable Valdyna Ogorkiewicz in her later years. Born in 1900, she was to remain the keystone of RMO's home life until she died in London in 1986 without having been able to return to her native Poland.

Chapter 2
Writer, lecturer and consultant in Britain

Newly elected to the Board of Trustees, RMO shows a Japanese tank- engineer acquaintance, Mr Tagaya, around The Tank Museum, Bovington in 1993. The group is flanked on the left by a Sherman and on the right by a Churchill tank, these happening to be the two types on which he cut his teeth during cadet training at the Army Technical School, Arborfield in 1943-45, while a teenaged mechanical engineering student at Imperial.

Although I became interested in tanks when I was still at school, I did not get into one until I became a cadet in the University of London Senior Training Corps, which I joined soon after I started my engineering studies at Imperial College. I then attended, in 1944, the first of three annual courses at what was at the time the Training Centre of the Royal Electrical and Mechanical Engineers (REME) at Arborfield in Berkshire and there I was also able to drive a tank for the first time. The courses provided very useful hands-on experience of working on typical tanks and in particular on the US-built Sherman medium tank and British Churchill infantry tank which were then being used by the British Army.

A year later I presented a student paper on tanks to the Engineering Society at Imperial College of which I was a member and in 1948 I wrote my first article on tanks which I submitted to the Royal Armoured Corps (RAC) Journal. The article was on Soviet tanks and produced an unexpected invitation to an interview at the War Office. It turned out that Military Intelligence were curious where I obtained all the information on which the article was based. But once they satisfied themselves that I was not using classified sources of information the interview ended amicably and the article was published in the RAC Journal in the following year.

In fact, the information on which this article as well as my other early writing was based came from a synthesis of

a wide variety of the available sources. They included what relevant books there were in the libraries of the Imperial War Museum and of the Institution of Mechanical Engineers (of which I was a Graduate Member and much later became a Fellow); documents left by the Polish forces in Britain given to me by my father; and information collected by following the Press.

So far as information about the history of the early armoured vehicles is concerned, I corresponded with at least one man who personally knew F.R. Simms, the engineer and entrepreneur who was responsible for the construction in 1902 of the very first vehicle that was both armed and armoured. The Simms Motor & Electronics Corporation which he founded in London also very kindly provided me with some hitherto unpublished information about it from its files. Further, I had the good fortune to correspond with and to meet Lieutenant Colonel Philip Johnson who led attempts during the latter part of the First World War to increase the speed of tanks. He subsequently designed the Medium D and Light Infantry tanks which attained maximum speeds of 20 and 30 miles per hour respectively, when the speed of most contemporary tanks was not more than about 7 miles per hour. I also visited Sir Harry Ricardo, who in 1916 designed the first engine built specifically for tanks and whose company at Shoreham in Sussex developed the first tank diesel engine in the 1920s.

Writing on tanks

After contributing my first article to the *RAC Journal* I wrote 29 more for it, some of which I even illustrated with Indian ink drawings of armoured vehicles mentioned in them.

COVENTRY I

As a budding contributor to the *RAC Journal* RMO demonstrated he was also an accomplished draughtsman by producing drawings to support his texts, such as these of the Daimler/Humber Coventry I armoured car and Renault's FT tank.

I also wrote several more articles for other British military journals, such as the *Army Quarterly* and the *Journal of the Royal United Service Institution*. I also contributed many articles to US defence journals, particularly to *ARMOR* and *Defense Review*, and to other military publications, ranging from *An Cosantoir*, the Irish defence journal, to the *Journal of the United Service Institution of India*. I also contributed several articles on tanks to *International Defense Review*, which was originally published by Interavia SA in Switzerland and of which I became eventually a consulting editor, and to *THE ENGINEER*, as well as contributing an entry on tanks to the *Encyclopaedia Britannica* and a chapter on them to

"Engineering Heritage", a book published in 1963 by the Institution of Mechanical Engineers. Altogether I must have written more than 500 articles on tanks and related subjects, which is probably more than anyone else had done during the 1950s and 1960s, and I believe they helped to make the characteristics and the capabilities of tanks and of other armoured vehicles more widely known.

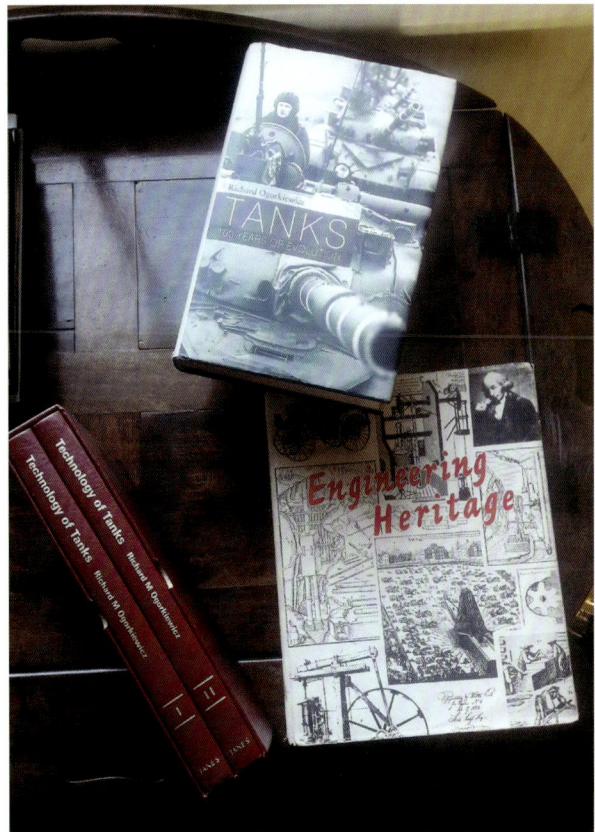

In addition to lecturing, consulting and writing hundreds of journal articles over a 70-year period, RMO authored or contributed to several books, among them "Engineering Heritage" (IME 1963), his own two-volume textbook "Technology of Tanks" (Jane's 1991), and his tank-centenary tour de force "Tanks – 100 years of evolution" (Osprey 2015).

The publication of my articles encouraged me to write my first book which was published in 1960 in Britain by Stevens and Sons and in the United States by Frederick Praeger under the title "Armour: the development of mechanised forces and their equipment". It happened to be the first comprehensive account of the subject published after the Second World War and as such it attracted considerable interest, including more than a dozen favourable reviews. It was also translated into Italian and published in Rome under the title "I Corazzati" by the *Instituto para la Divulgazione della Storia Militare* and in 1970 it was republished in Britain under the title "Armoured Forces" by Arms and Armour Press.

By then I had written a second book entitled "Design and Development of Fighting Vehicles" which was published in 1968 in Britain by Macdonald and in the United States by Doubleday. Like the first, it was well received and attracted favourable reviews as well as being translated into Japanese and published in Tokyo in 1983.

My third book, entitled "Technology of Tanks", was not published until 1991 when the Cold War had come to an end and the First Gulf War had just taken place. These events led to a decline of interest in tanks and this adversely affected the sales of the book, which were further aggravated by its unnecessarily expensive two-volume format adopted by its publishers. However, I found several years after its publication that the book remained in demand and that available copies were selling at ten times its original price! A more reasonably priced version was produced in Austria in 1998 in a German translation, entitled "Technologie der Panzer".

Several years later I wrote another book entitled "Tanks: 100 years of evolution" which was published in 2015, on the centenary of the construction of the first tank. It was followed by its Polish translation, entitled "Czolgi: sto lat historii", which was published in Warsaw in 2016 and a Russian translation published in 2019.

Much of my books and many of my articles were concerned with the development of tanks and other armoured vehicles but I also ventured into the arena of debates about the role of tanks and the organization of armoured formations. In particular, I argued against the view that tanks should be divided into two separate categories of "infantry" and "cavalry" tanks. This view was widely held before the Second World War and persisted for a time after it, particularly in Britain, perpetuating a historical model that was made invalid by technology. In spite of this, as late as 1950 two of the pioneers of tank warfare, Generals J.F.C. Fuller and G.le Q. Martel, still argued in letters to The Times that there should be the two categories of tanks.

I also argued against the doctrine, to which British and US armies adhered during the Second World War, that the role of the armoured divisions should be confined to the exploitation of successes won by other arms. In fact, starting with the German panzer divisions, armoured divisions proved to be versatile and highly effective fighting formations.

Based on the study of the operations of the mixed, tank-mechanised infantry battle groups, or Kampfgruppen, employed by the German Army during the later stages of the Second World War I argued, particularly in my first book, that the organization of armoured forces should be based on integrated, tank-infantry armoured battle groups. My advocacy of such an organization attracted attention at the Pentagon when in the post-Vietnam era General J. Kalergis was appointed to draw up plans for the reorganization of the US Army. I was invited to a meeting with General Kalergis to discuss the battle group concept but it was not accepted at the time. However, it has been widely adopted since then.

In my early writing I advocated the development of lighter tanks and in an article published in 1957 I proposed that, instead of guns, some of them be armed with anti-tank guided missiles which were just beginning to be produced, in France. However, in Britain there was scepticism at the time about the lethality of their shaped-charge warheads, even after the pioneering French SS.10 missile was finally tested in 1958. My proposal was clearly at odds with official opinion, as were some of my other ideas, so much so that the Director of the Fighting Vehicles Research and Development Establishment (FVRDE) jokingly greeted me on one occasion as his "principal enemy"!

A French Army AMX-13 light tank fitted with an early version of the 3,000m-range Nord Aviation SS.11 missile to bolster its 75mm gun in the tank-destroyer role. Unlike their French, Russian and US contemporaries, British officials were not persuaded of the efficacy of hybrid gun/missile armament solutions – though the SS.11 itself was successfully used from British forces' Scout helicopters in the 1982 Falklands War. (French Army)

FVRDE became the site of the first major display of British Army equipment, which I attended in 1961. One of its features was the first public appearance of a prototype of the Chieftain tank which represented a major advance in tank design and became the Western World's most heavily armed and armoured battle tank. I promoted it in some of my articles and lectures, partly to support the Defence Sales branch of the Ministry of Defence which was trying to attract orders for it from allied countries. However, I remained sceptical of the complicated ammunition system of its 120mm rifled gun which, unlike that of other tank guns, consisted of three parts - projectile, bagged propellant charge and igniter (or 'vent tube') - that had to be brought together for the gun to function.

Photograph of a Chieftain prototype gracing the cover of the pilot edition of Interavia's *International Defense Review*, first published in 1965. RMO went on to write 172 features for this publication between 1970-2015.

FVRDE was also the site of five exhibitions of British military vehicles held at intervals from 1954 to 1971, but only the last two of which included tanks. The presentation of armoured fighting vehicles then shifted to the British Army Equipment Exhibition which was held in the 1970s at Aldershot, the home of British Army, and which became an important showcase of the development of armoured vehicles in Britain.

In 1948, soon after I started writing articles, I made the first of my many visits to The Tank Museum at Bovington in Dorset where I could study its unique collection of the original, World War I tanks as well as some more recently produced armoured vehicles. My visits led eventually to being elected, in 1987, President of the Friends of the Museum for the first of two three-year terms and in 1993 I was voted onto the Board of Trustees of the Museum, on which I then served for 25 years.

During the years I served as a trustee of the Museum, it acquired an additional wing which the Queen opened in 2009, when I was presented to her together with the other trustees. The expansion of the Museum provided an opportunity for a re-arrangement of the display of the tanks and other armoured vehicles in it, and this became the subject of considerable debate in which I participated. I advocated according a maximum of prominence, in their own right, to the most important of the vehicles in the Museum and not using them as mere props or 'wallpaper' in the Museum's popular exhibitions.

RMO is presented to HM Queen Elizabeth II together with other trustees during her visit to The Tank Museum in 2009. (Tank Museum)

One of the vehicles in the Museum which deserved being prominently displayed was the Hornsby tractor, the oldest surviving tracked tractor in the world which the British Army paraded at Aldershot as early as 1910 and which was the forerunner, albeit indirectly, of the first British tanks built five years later. Another outstanding vehicle that should be prominently displayed has been the Vickers Medium tank which, in the 1920s inspired the development of faster tanks around the world and which constituted the basis on which the Royal Tank Corps pioneered the evolution of the tactics of mobile tank warfare. A tank which also deserves prominence is the A.1, or Independent, that, in spite of its four questionable auxiliary machine gun turrets, constituted in the early 1920s a major advance in the configuration of tanks. It became a model for the A.6, or Sixteen Tonner, which was claimed to be the acme of British tank development before the Second World War.

The forerunner of the tank: the Hornsby tractor, the first fully tracked commercial design to have been built in Britain, was trialled by the British Army between 1905-1907. A smaller version, built to a military specification, was tested in 1910-11.

The Vickers Medium tank, which had a turreted 47mm main gun and a top speed in excess of 20 mph.

I also argued that the Museum's original First World War tanks, which are unique to it and which account for much of its historical importance and world reputation, should not be be dispersed but be prominently displayed together.

All such debates aside, my many years of association with the Museum also led me to a decision to bequeath my collection of books, documents and papers dealing with tanks and other armoured vehicles to its Archives.

The prototype 32-ton multi-turreted A1 Independent tank constructed by Vickers in 1926.

Sir Basil Liddell Hart.

My early visits to The Tank Museum involved helping officers at what was then the School of Tank Technology, also located at the Royal Armoured Corps Centre and responsible at the time for running the Museum, to collect information about tanks for the history of the Royal Tank Regiment (RTR) which Captain B.H. Liddell Hart (later Sir Basil Liddell Hart), the world-famous military thinker and writer, was asked to write. This took several years but when the two-volume history of the RTR was published in 1959 under the title "The Tanks" Liddell Hart very generously acknowledged in it my help.

In the meantime Liddell Hart invited me to contribute a chapter on Soviet tanks to a collective work entitled "The Soviet Army" and published in 1956 by Weidenfeld & Nicolson which he edited. I had by then met him in person and began to correspond with him frequently as well as visiting him at his house at Wolverton Park in Buckinghamshire, particularly when I was working in Coventry and could stop on Friday evenings en route to week-ends with my parents in London. He was very hospitable and I would stop for discussions over dinner and even stay overnight on occasion.

The discussions as well as the correspondence inevitably revolved around the development of mechanised forces and armoured warfare. Among others, he generously shared with me information little known at the time about German armoured forces during the Second World War, which was given to him by several German generals in response to his chivalrous attitude to them when they were vindictively held as prisoners of war for a number of years after the end of hostilities.

Liddell Hart liked to dwell on the fact that in his early writing he advocated including some infantry in the composition of the armoured formations, if only as "tank marines", in contrast to others, like General Fuller, who wrote of what were essentially "all tank" forces. He also encouraged claims made on his behalf that the successful "blitzkrieg" of the German armoured forces in France in 1940 was influenced directly by some of his ideas but the claims were questionable and did more harm than good to his worldwide reputation which was high enough without them.

I visited Liddell Hart again several times when he moved to Medmenham near Marlow in Buckinghamshire. After he died suddenly in 1970 I kept in touch for a number of years with his charming wife, Kathleen, who loyally supported him in his activities and zealously guarded his reputation.

Consultant to industry

When my writings became widely known, I was invited by a number of companies involved in the development of tanks to become an advisor to them. The first was Marconi Command and Control Systems of Leicester, with which, from 1976 onwards, I became involved in the development of tank fire and gun control systems, not only for tanks being developed in Britain but also in other countries, including Greece which involved visiting the Technical Directorate of the Greek Army in Athens in 1977. It also included accompanying a delegation of the Chinese Peoples Liberation Army (PLA) visiting, for the first time, Marconi in Leicester and the British Army's tank gunnery school at Lulworth in Dorset. The programme of the visit included a day for sightseeing in London but the delegation opted instead to have me lecture to them on tanks! To complete the friendly occasion I was presented, after the lecture, with an interesting, woven picture of a section of the Great Wall.

Another company which invited me, in 1982, to become an adviser was Vickers Defence Systems, of Newcastle upon Tyne, Britain's longest-established tank producer. A year later I became involved in a major competitive future tank design study funded by the Ministry of Defence at Vickers and two other armoured vehicle-producing companies, namely Alvis and Royal Ordnance. The study brought out some interesting ideas but none of them was adopted. While working with Vickers, I wrote several reports including one produced for their managing director in response to a proposal to use a gas turbine in the next British tank, in which I argued at some length why a gas turbine engine should not be used.

The modernised 'straight-through' tank production facility opened by Vickers at its Scotswood, Newcastle plant in the early 1980s to handle small-batch production of its Mk3 export tank and engineer vehicles for Nigeria. The plant was subsequently duplicated in Leeds as part of the contractual obligations surrounding Vickers' takeover of the Royal Ordnance Factories' Challenger production operation in 1986. However the latter site was shut in 2004 when the (by-then) Alvis Vickers company was subsumed within the newly formed BAe Systems Land Systems organization. In 2012 BAe decided that the Scotswood plant should similarly be closed. Some Challenger 2 tank repair work resumed there in 2015 after the site had been acquired by the Reece Group, which includes armoured engineer systems specialists Pearson Engineering. (Vickers)

My consulting activities at Vickers and Marconi continued until the early 1990s when, after the end of the Cold War and the collapse of the Soviet Union, defence budgets and work on armoured vehicles were drastically reduced as part of the so-called "Peace Dividend". One of the consequences was the closing down of Britain's tank producing factories. Thus, the Alvis light armoured vehicle factory in Coventry was demolished and replaced by a shopping complex, while the Royal Ordnance tank factory in Leeds became an industrial estate. The last to go was Vickers' factory in Newcastle which was closed in 2012. This was preceded ten years earlier by the delivery of the last tank to be built in Britain, a Challenger 2, and together with the subsequent closure of the Vickers factory, marked an end of the ability of Britain to produce tanks which it enjoyed for almost one hundred years.

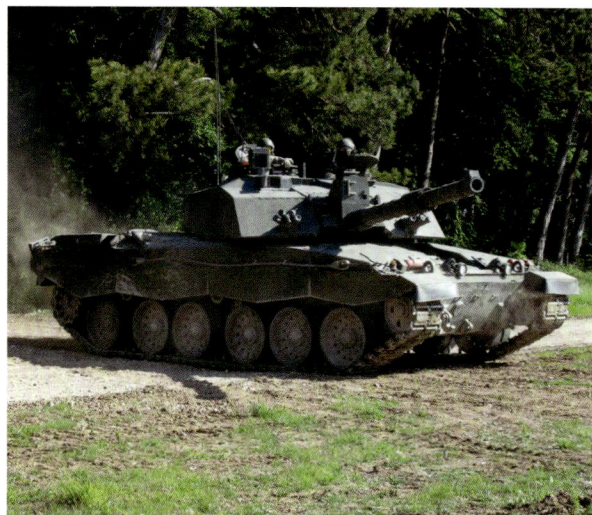

Challenger 2 – the last tank to be designed and built in Britain. (R Pengelley)

While still a consultant to Marconi and Vickers, I also acted for shorter periods of time as a consultant to a number of other British companies. One of them was Racal Radar Defence Systems, for which I wrote, between 1982 and 1985, reports on their Saviour radar and laser threat warning system and its possible combination with 'soft kill' countermeasures. Such a system was not adopted for British tanks but it subsequently emerged that a 'soft kill' defence system, called Shtora, was being developed by the Soviet Army against anti-tank guided missiles and it appeared on some Soviet tanks in the early 1990s. Another British company to which I was a consultant during the 1980s was Mantell Technical Services, which was involved in modifying Soviet-produced armoured vehicles acquired by the Egyptian Army. This led to it being visited in 1982 by a group of Egyptian Army officers and I was asked to give a presentation to them on armoured vehicle development, which I did in one of London's leading hotels.

In the mid-1980s I also supported a proposal to the Ministry of Defence by Royal Ordnance to produce under licence the six-wheeled Pandur armoured carrier which had been developed in Austria by the Steyr Daimler Puch company. This would have provided relatively quickly an up to date wheeled armoured carrier which the Army needed for its mechanised infantry. But the idea was rejected. Instead the Ministry of Defence ordered the four-wheeled GKN Saxon carrier, which was little more than a cheap armoured truck. Eventually some were palmed off on the Ukraine, while a commander of the British land forces called them "useless".

Steyr's Pandur 6x6 in its armoured reconnaissance scout vehicle version, armed with a 25mm cannon.

However, in 1995 the Ministry of Defence entered into an agreement with German and French authorities for jointly developing a Multi Role Armoured Vehicle, or MRAV - a wheeled armoured personnel carrier in effect. The French Army pulled out of the agreement in 1999 to develop more quickly its own eight-wheeled Véhicule Blindé de Combat d'Infanterie (VBCI), which it successfully deployed on operations in Afghanistan from 2010 and in Mali from 2013. The German and British armies persevered with MRAV but it was becoming large and heavy. This led me to question its ability to operate effectively on soft, wet soils in spite of its large tyres, and my comments resulted in some tests on such soils. But the tests proved inconclusive and became irrelevant so far as the British Army was concerned as it withdrew from the MRAV programme in 2003.
It then made no serious effort for more than a decade to provide its mechanised infantry with multi-wheeled armoured carriers - in contrast to almost every other army of any consequence.

Almost before I became an industrial consultant I was invited, in 1972, to join the Land Warfare Advisory Board of the Defence Scientific Advisory Council (DSAC) of the Ministry of Defence and was to serve on the various boards and committees of the DSAC until 2006.

Early prototype of the multilateral GTK/MRAV 8x8, alias Boxer, in its infantry carrier configuration. The UK was a founding partner in the programme in the 1990s, but pulled out in 2003 in pursuit of the abortive FRES programme, only to re-adopt Boxer in 2018. (Krauss Maffei)

Tank guns

MAIN ARMAMENT
105MM M68 GUN

The Royal Ordnance L7 105mm 52-calibre rifled gun found wide acceptance within NATO, this US-produced M68A1E2 variant with a vertical sliding-block breech being selected as the main armament for the initial version of the M1 Abrams tank.

Soon after beginning to serve on the DSAC I became involved in a debate in the Ministry of Defence about future tank guns. At the time the 105mm L7 rifled gun firing armour-piercing hard-cored discarding sabot (APDS) ammunition, which was developed in Britain, dominated the Western tank world. In fact, almost all Western tanks built from the 1960s well into the 1980s, from Japan to Argentina as well as the United States, Germany, Sweden and Israel - and even Chinese tanks - were armed with these guns, albeit modified in some cases. The APDS ammunition, which was responsible for much of the success of the 105mm L7 and its derivatives, is generally thought to have originated in Britain when, in fact, it had begun to be developed in France before the Second World War, at the Edgar Brandt armament company famous for its infantry mortars. When France was being overrun by the German forces in 1940, some of the Brandt engineers escaped to Britain bringing with them the results of their preliminary work. This was taken up at the Armament Research and Development Establishment at Fort Halstead in Kent, which led to the production of the first tank gun to use APDS ammunition - the 57mm 6pdr gun of the British Churchill tank - and the subsequent development of other British tank guns using similar ammunition.

However, in 1972 I took part in a study in the United States, commissioned by the US Defense Advanced Research Projects Agency (DARPA) to assess the effectiveness of various anti-tank weapons. This concluded that the most effective of them were going to be "high-velocity guns firing APFSDS (armour piercing fin-stabilised discarding sabot) projectiles" - that is, projectiles with long, arrow-like, fin-stabilised penetrators. I contributed to and fully endorsed that conclusion, which led me in the following year to raise the superiority of APFSDS over APDS in a personal letter to the Master General of the Ordnance. He happened to be away at the time but I received a friendly reply from his Deputy that spin-stabilised APDS would continue to be superior to the fin-stabilised APFSDS! Those involved in British tank-gun development were apparently unwilling to concede that the APDS, with which they had been so successful, could be improved upon by another type of ammunition.

It took a tripartite firing trial - British, US and German - carried out three years later to demonstrate clearly the superiority of APFSDS, and from then on the latter began to be generally recognised as the most effective type of armour piercing, tank gun ammunition.

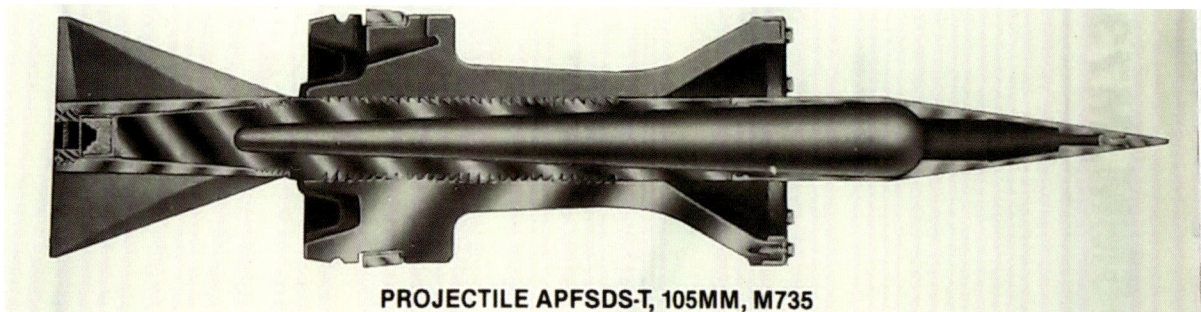

PROJECTILE APFSDS-T, 105MM, M735

Cutaway of the US M735 105mm APFSDS-T projectile with its multi-part long-rod penetrator containing a sheathed tungsten core. This proved it could out-penetrate and match in accuracy the heavier British 120mm APDS sub-projectile when engaging the NATO heavy triple target during the Trilateral Gun Trials staged at Shoeburyness in 1975.

However, other debates about tank guns continued. In 1980 a new tank began to be considered to succeed the British Army's Chieftain, that would retain the latter's 120mm rifled gun. I argued at a meeting at the Ministry of Defence with three senior scientific civil servants involved in tank development that the new tank should instead be armed with a more powerful 120mm smoothbore gun firing APFSDS ammunition, which had been developed in Germany by the Rheinmetall company.

A classic Leopard 2A4 tank, fitted with the baseline L44 version of Rheinmetall's 120mm smoothbore gun, which was adopted for the US Army's M1A1/2 Abrams tank models as the M256.

This gun had just been adopted for the new German Leopard 2 tank and had been selected to arm future versions of the US M1 tank so, apart from its specific merits, its adoption would have had the advantage of British tanks using the same gun and ammunition as its principal allies. However, my arguments were dismissed on the grounds that the Rheinmetall gun could not be adopted without major and costly modifications to the turrets of the new tank and of the 700-odd Chieftains which were expected to remain in use for some time. The merits of the 120mm Rheinmetall gun were resurrected twenty years later when one was installed in a Challenger 2 tank but even then nothing was done about adopting it.

In the meantime the Rheinmetall gun was adopted in several other countries for new tanks, becoming the Western World's standard tank gun just as the 105mm rifled gun had been, and Britain thus lost the lead in tank gun development which it had previously enjoyed.

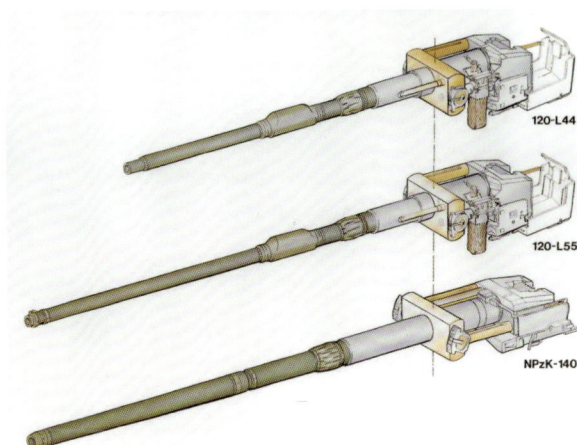

Rheinmetall's growth path for the Leopard 2 main armament solution originally extended from the L44 and L55 versions of its 120mm smoothbore gun to its NPzK-140. This was the German iteration of the successor 140mm smoothbore developed in harmony with the Americans, British, and French under the quadrilateral Future Tank Main Armament (FTMA) programme.

By 1990 I also became involved, in and out of the DSAC, in discussions about novel tank gun systems. These included guns using liquid instead of conventional, solid propellants which had been considered, on and off, since the 1950s. But before the latest version could be fully developed liquid propellant guns came to be considered more suitable for artillery than for tanks and work on them was then discontinued, first in Britain and finally, in 1995, in the United States.

More than 20 years after RMO's arguments in favour of the German 120mm smoothbore for the Chieftain's successor were rejected on grounds of cost, a hybrid version of Rheinmetall's 120mm L55 gun was successfully installed aboard this Challenger 2 as a potential 'spend to save' measure under the 2003-06 Challenger Lethality Improvement Programme (CLIP). No funds could be found for CLIP implementation at the time, but in 2019 the Rheinmetall 120mm L55 smoothbore gun was once again selected in principle for a renewed round of Challenger 2 modernisation, matched to a new turret. (UK MoD)

The barrel of one of two American rail gun-type EM launcher systems installed at Kirkcudbright for testing projectiles at tank-like muzzle energies (9-10MJ) and at double the normal velocities (up to 3,000m/s). This version, made by IAP Research Inc, had a 90mm bore and a length of 7m. (UK MoD)

Another departure from conventional solid-propellant guns took the form of electro-magnetic (EM) guns, which offered the prospect of much higher projectile velocities as well as other potential advantages. Work on them began in the United States in the early 1980s and was taken up a few years later in Britain, where there was talk already at the 3rd European Symposium on Electromagnetic Launch Technology held in London in 1991 of mounting an EM gun on a Chieftain tank chassis.

Interest in EM guns led, among others, to the construction of an Anglo-American electro-magnetic launch facility at the firing range at Kirkcudbright in Scotland, which I had an opportunity of visiting in 1993 as a member of a DSAC working party on the novel gun systems. My view at the time was that the prospect of electro-magnetic launchers being transformed into tank guns was "somewhat remote".

The Ministry of Defence was more optimistic, as in the late 1990s it embarked on studies of a tank with an EM gun which was called MODIFIER (Mobile Direct Fire Equipment Requirement) and was expected to come into service in 2020.

However, nothing came of this because in 1999 the US Army decided to transform itself into a strategically more mobile, air transportable force. This implied the use of armoured vehicles that could be carried in aircraft like the Lockheed C-130 Hercules and could not therefore weigh more than about 19 tonnes, which ruled out any prospect of the use of tanks armed with electro-magnetic guns because of the weight and size of their electrical systems.

The aspirations of the US Army became embodied in its Future Combat Systems (FCS) programme and came to be shared to some extent by the British Army's Future Rapid Effect System (FRES) programme which was inspired by it. But FRES was even more questionable than FCS because of the limitations of the available airlift capability. The latter became the subject of a DSAC working party, which I chaired and which brought out in its report the obvious lack in Britain of aircraft capable of carrying any of the existing armoured vehicles. After this I chaired, in 2002, one more DSAC working party, this time on future ground platforms which confirmed the continued need for manned, protected, ground weapon platforms or, in other words, tanks.

The report of my working party was issued by the Defence Science and Technology Laboratory (DSTL), which in 2001 took over what was left of the Defence Evaluation and Research Agency (DERA) of the Ministry of Defence after most of it was hived off to QinetiQ and other private companies. Before DERA was broken up, it commissioned a collective work which would be a record of the defence research in Britain between 1945 and 1990 and I was asked to contribute to it a chapter on armoured fighting vehicles. The resulting book was published in 1999 by the Science Museum in London under the title "Cold War, Hot Science".

Soon after beginning to serve on the DSAC, I was invited to give a lecture on tanks to the Army Staff Course at the Royal Military College of Science (RMCS), Shrivenham. The lecture took place in 1979 and was attended by all three Divisions of the Course immediately before the end-of-course speech by the Master General of the Ordnance. It must have proved of interest as I was asked to repeat it in the following four years. When the Army Staff Course was later reorganized and split up, I continued to lecture to other courses. In 1988 I was appointed, a Visiting Professor at RMCS, and six years later I was also made an Honorary Fellow of the School of Mechanical, Materials and Civil Engineering at the College.

The various courses in which I lectured ranged from one on Military Vehicle Technology to another on Fundamentals of Armour Protection, and gradually changed from their emphasis on battle tanks during the Cold War to lighter vehicles used in the contemporary counter-insurgency operations in the Middle East. Among others, I set up a Fundamentals of Armour Protection Course in collaboration with Professor Manfred Held, the inventor of explosive reactive armour, whom I met at the 13th International Symposium on Ballistics in Stockholm in 1992 and who was prepared to fly in from Munich, where he lived, to lecture when required. This he did for several years and his untimely death in 2011 was a severe loss to the Course, which came to an end soon afterwards when I had to give up lecturing for health reasons. By then the RMCS had been re-branded the Defence Academy of the United Kingdom and the symposia and courses on armoured vehicles which were held at it had lost their international standing or simply ceased, as did the development of tanks in Britain.

At about the same time, I also gave up participating in the various business conferences on armoured vehicles held in London since the 1980s. One of the earliest of them was a US-sponsored conference on "Battlefield Weapons Systems" held in 1980 in London, at the Royal Aeronautical Society, and in Munich, at which I spoke on "Combat vehicles in

NATO". In 1983 I also spoke at a conference on "Western Arms Co-operation" held in London by *The Economist* magazine and I took part in a conference on "Special Operations" run in 1991 in London and Brussels by Advanced Technology International, to which I contributed a paper on "Armoured Vehicles in Low Intensity Conflicts" that were then beginning to come to the fore.

I then helped to set up in 1992 in London the first of four Shephard "Armoured Warfare" conferences. This was distinguished by the attendance of a Russian general, reflecting a temporary improvement in British-Russian relations following the end of the Cold War. In 1998 I started attending, until 2006, SMI's "Armour and Anti-Armour" conferences, some of which I chaired. I also attended, from their inception in 2003 until 2010, IQPC conferences on " Light and Medium Armoured Vehicles". The business conferences were at first held in hotels or similar premises, but as they grew in popularity they migrated to larger conference facilities, including the ExCel Centre in London's Dockland, and they provided useful if general reviews of the developments in tanks and other armoured vehicles.

In addition to attending different business conferences I took part, from 1995 onwards, in the "European Fighting Vehicle Symposia" at RMCS, at one of which I gave the keynote address and to which, among others, I managed to attract speakers from the Japanese Mitsubishi company and from the Turkish Otokar company. In 2001 and 2002 I also presented papers on "Future Combat Vehicles" at conferences at the Royal United Services Institute in London, in which I re-stated my faith in tanks, whatever their future shape or form might be.

Chapter 3
Following development of tanks and other armoured vehicles in Western Europe

My initial connection with developments in Western Europe and specifically in West Germany was through Dr. Ferdinand von Senger und Etterlin. He was a *Panzerwaffe* officer and as such fought during the Second World War on the Eastern Front, including Stalingrad, being wounded during the fighting and losing his right arm. After the War he studied law at Oxford University, where he was a Rhodes Scholar, and at universities in Germany. When I met him he was working on reviving the tradition of the "Taschenbuch der Tanks", a series of books on tanks and other armoured vehicles written by an Austrian officer, Captain Fritz Heigl.

These were the first and only books published during the 1920s to contain a comprehensive account of them and remained a source of detailed information until a year or two before the Second World. Von Senger's successor publication was given the slightly different title of "Taschenbuch der Panzer" but it was printed in 1954 by the same publisher, J.F. Lehmanns Verlag of Munich, as had published Heigl's first book 28 years earlier. I was able to give von Senger some help in its preparation and he generously acknowledged it in the book's introduction.

I also contributed to a book by von Senger entitled "Die Panzer Grenadiere" which was published in 1961. It was the first book to be written specifically on armoured or mechanized infantry and my contribution to it consisted of sections dealing with developments in Britain, France and the United States

By the time the first edition of "Taschenbuch der Panzer" was published, I had started a lively correspondence with von Senger about tanks and the organization of armoured forces. This went on for almost 20 years, during which he visited me in London and I revisited him and his family in 1963 with my mother when I took her on a motor tour of the Netherlands and West Germany.

By then the German Army had been recreated and von Senger had joined it when this happened in 1956, becoming involved some time afterwards in the trials of the pre-production version of the new German Leopard 1 tank. But in 1964 he assumed command of a tank battalion which was still equipped with US-built M48 tanks and had to be

transported that year for its annual gunnery training to a British Army firing range at Castlemartin on the south coast of Wales because all the ranges in Germany were already fully used by other NATO tank units! I took advantage of it to visit him at Castlemartin and he gave me an opportunity to examine one of the M48 tanks of his battalion and to fire from it.

An early-production Leopard 1, with its cast turret progressively upgraded in the 1970s and 80s to A1A1 standard with appliqué armour and night-vision equipment mounts, is today consigned as a gateguard at the Castlemartin range in Wales, where German Army crews were sent for gunnery training during the Cold War. (R Pengelley)

Von Senger eventually became a general and Commander-in-Chief of NATO Allied Forces Central Europe and retired in 1983. In the meantime on his advice I contacted a number of German companies involved in the development and production of armoured vehicles. The principal one was the Krauss-Maffei company in Munich, which was producing the newly developed Leopard 1 tank. After some years of correspondence, it invited me in 1969 to a specially arranged demonstration of a Leopard 1 which I was able to drive and view in production. Compared with some other contemporary tanks I found it easy to drive and I became impressed with the high quality of the detailed engineering I observed within it, particularly in the tank's power pack. On the following day I made another interesting visit, in Munich-Ottobrunn, to Messerschmitt-Bolkow-Blohm, the leading German missile company at the time, which invited me to acquaint myself with some of its activities.

A prototype of the German/US MBT-70 tank, out of whose demise the Leopard 2 was born. MBT-70 was unusual in having the driver seated within the turret, and incorporated the XM150 152mm combined gun/missile launcher. (US Army)

I was invited again to Munich in 1971 and 1976 for discussions at Krauss-Maffei and became involved in promoting, by writing articles about it and in discussions, a successor to Leopard 1 called Leopard 2AV, or "Austere Version". The latter was developed, after the fiasco of the US-German MBT-70 tank programme, to compete with the XM1 tank which was subsequently designed in the United States, for possible adoption as the one tank that would be used by both the US and German armies. However nothing came of this idea, each country eventually adopting its own candidate. But Leopard 2AV was successfully developed into Leopard 2 for the German Army and was produced for it and later also for several other armies, becoming the Western world's most widely used tank.

I was invited to Munich in 1979 to attend the ceremony of the formal handing over of the first Leopard 2 to the German Army, which was preceded by a comprehensive one-day conference about the tank's features at the mountain resort of Garmisch-Partenkirchen. I then kept in contact with and visited Krauss-Maffei over a period of about 20 years following its development of Leopard 2 and other armoured vehicles. During this period I regarded Leopard 2 as the best tank in the Western world and said so in 1989, when interviewed on BBC television and elsewhere at the time that the British Army was trying to decide what tank to adopt to succeed Challenger 1.

Whichever the tank, I also favoured the Rheinmetall 120mm L44 smoothbore gun of Leopard 2, as described in Chapter 2. This gun was originally developed as a potential alternative to the 152mm gun/missile launcher of the ill-fated US-German MBT-70 but, after the latter was abandoned, it was adopted for Leopard 2 and from 1985 for the second version of the US M1 Abrams, the M1A1, as the 120mm M256. The adoption of the Rheinmetall gun by the US Army was somewhat ironic because its design actually originated in the United States with the experimental 120mm smoothbore Delta gun which the US Army was developing in the early 1960s but abandoned when it became enamoured with guided-missile launchers as tank armament, leaving the development and production of this type of gun to Germany.

In 1981 I was invited to visit Rheinmetall in Dusseldorf to see some of its facilities and to discuss its development of the low recoil-force version of the widely used, British-designed 105mm L7 tank gun which could be fired from vehicles weighing as little as 14 tonnes. This Rheinmetall Rh 105-11 gun overtook the 75mm Ares gun which was being developed in the United States for lightweight combat vehicles, as mentioned in Chapter 4, and led to the construction in several countries of experimental light tanks of 20 - 30 tonnes, based generally on the chassis of infantry armoured fighting vehicles which were armed with similar, low recoil-force 105mm tank guns.

The visits to Krauss-Maffei in Munich also led me to contacts with the Renk transmission gears company which, among others, was producing the transmission for Leopard 2. Tank transmissions and in particular the tracked-vehicle steering mechanisms which they incorporated always intrigued me and I enjoyed discussing them at Renk which was in the forefront of their development. The transmission which Renk was producing for Leopard 2 and other tracked armoured vehicles was of the hydro-mechanical type which began to come into use after the Second World War, superseding the earlier, purely mechanical transmission still used in some tanks designed after the Second World War, like the British Chieftain.

While hydro-mechanical transmissions became the norm in Western tanks, there appeared on the horizon a potential alternative to them, in the form of electric transmissions. Sporadic attempts to use such transmissions were made during the First and Second World Wars, but thereafter interest in them lay dormant until the 1960s. Some of the credit for the revival of interest goes to the Atelier de Constructions Electriques de Charleroi (ACEC) in Belgium who installed an experimental electric transmission in a modified, US-built M24 light tank. During a visit to Belgium I was given a test ride in the ACEC-modified M24 tank which clearly demonstrated the potential of electric tank transmissions.

Growing interest in electric transmissions contributed to the setting up of the 1st International Conference on All-Electric Combat Vehicles which I attended in Haifa, Israel, in 1995. Two years later I attended another All-Electric Combat Vehicles (AECV) conference, this time in the United States, in Detroit, and later still others in Angers, France; Bath in Britain and in 2007 in Stockholm, Sweden. The latter turned out to be the last of the international conferences of their kind, not because of a loss of faith in the future of electric tank transmissions but because of a general decline in the resources devoted to tank development brought about by the end of the Cold War.

Magnet Motor's 8x8 electric transmission demonstrator. (Magnet Motor)

In 1991 and 1992 while there was still considerable activity related to electric transmissions, I visited the Magnet Motor company at Starnberg, in Germany. The latter was in the forefront of the development of electric transmissions and built experimental tracked and wheeled armoured vehicles fitted with them. The object of my visits was not only to acquaint myself with the transmissions which Magnet Motor had built but also to bring them to the notice of companies to which I was a consultant, and in particular General Dynamics Defense Systems and Vickers Defence. For similar reasons I also visited in 1991 GEC Alsthom at Lyon, in France, where it had designed some electric transmissions for tanks to French military requirements.

At about the same time I was invited by the MaK company to visit it in Kiel to see the armoured vehicles it was developing. MaK had shared some of the production of Leopard 2 with Krauss-Maffei but, by the time I was invited to visit, it was completing the production of the Weasel (*Wiesel*) light armoured carrier and, in collaboration with the Italian Oto Breda company, was developing the AV 90 tracked armoured infantry vehicle, both of which I was able to test drive. Weasel was particularly interesting as it only weighed 2.8 tonnes, which made it the lightest tracked armoured vehicle of its generation and transportable in heavy lift helicopters.

MTU's first-generation MB838 820hp V-10 diesel engine adopted for the Leopard 1 (MTU)

In between my visits to other German companies I also visited, several times, MTU, or Motoren und Turbinen Union, a company created by a merger of the high-performance diesel engine divisions of Mercedes Benz and Maybach and located at Friedrichshafen on Lake Constance. Having been involved with diesel engines I was very glad to be able to observe their progressive development by MTU, which started with a robust, water-cooled V-8 engine for the Swiss Pz.61 tank and continued with its V-10 development for the German Leopard 1.

The second-generation MTU MB873 1,500hp V-12 was originally destined for the German (KPz70) version of MBT-70 and subsequently switched to the Leopard 2. (MTU)

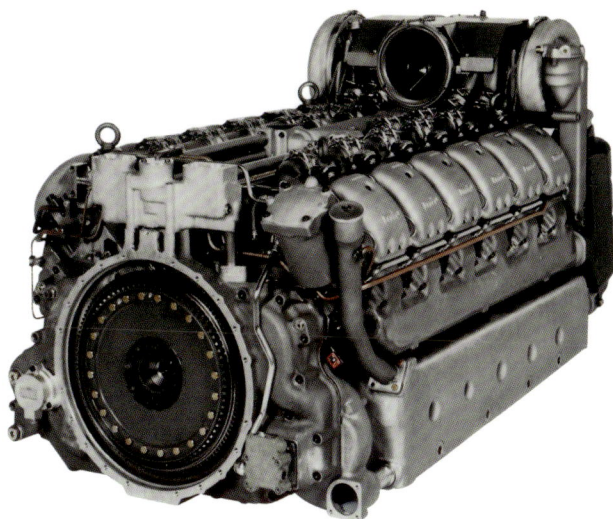

MTU's third-generation 1,500hp diesel, the MT883 V-12, was much more compact than its predecessor, and was taken up for the Israeli Merkava 4 tank as well as export versions of the British Challenger 2 and French Leclerc tanks among many others. (MTU)

These engines were followed by the second generation of MTU diesels, the most important of which was the MB 873 V-12 engine adopted for Leopard 2. They were followed in turn by the third generation of MTU engines, developed on the company's own initiative. These were led by the MT 883 which was much more compact than the earlier V-12 engines and more efficient thermodynamically, particularly in its direct-injection form. As a result it was adopted for the re-engined, export versions of some existing tanks such as the US M1 and British Challenger and for several new tanks, including the Israeli Merkava Mk 4.

In fact, MT 883 came to be regarded as the best of the contemporary tank engines and as such demonstrated the wisdom of a policy of developing progressively a well established type of engine, instead of trying to develop novel and unproven types, as was attempted several times in Britain, France and the United States.

My visits to Germany brought me into contact with Rolf Hilmes, who was Director of Studies, Land Weapon Systems, at the Federal Academy of Defence Administration and Technology in Mannheim. He was also the author of several books and numerous articles on tanks and other armoured vehicles. Hilmes invited me in 1995 to contribute to a symposium at the Academy which, unfortunately, I was not able to do but in the following year I visited Mannheim and Hilmes personally drove me to the German Army's tank training centre and The tank museum in Munster. On the way back we stopped in Koblenz to see the collection of armoured vehicles at the technical studies centre of the German Ministry of Defence. I visited Mannheim again in 2005 to speak at the Academy during a symposium on light armoured vehicles and afterwards to visit the technical museum at Sinsheim. I made no further visits after this to Mannheim but I continued to correspond regularly and exchange information with Hilmes.

France

Well before my visits to Germany I renewed my acquaintance with France. In fact, I revisited Paris in 1949, only four years after the end of the Second World War, and again in 1952, as well as in 1959 on my way back from a visit to Italy. None of these visits related directly to my interest in armoured vehicles but I took advantage of them to visit military as well as other museums and to rummage through bookshops in search of publications on the history of French tanks.

By about 1963 I established contact with the military attaché at the French embassy in London who very kindly helped me acquire some information about the post-Second World War development of armoured vehicles in France. He also helped me to arrange visits in 1966 to the Armoured Force and Cavalry School at Saumur on the Loire and to the Atelier de Construction d'Issy-les-Moulineaux (AMX), the centre for development of French tanks at Satory near Versailles.

The visit to Saumur proved to be very interesting as well as friendly, as it included viewing the collection of historic vehicles which were stored there pending the creation of a French tank museum, that I was to visit several times in later years. In return for the reception accorded to me by the School at Saumur I presented to its library a rare pre-Second World War book on French tanks which I acquired in the course of my search for historical material and which the School had lost.

When the AMX 30B model entered service in 1966, it was the most lightly protected tank of its generation. This picture shows an AMX 30B2 version three decades later, fortified against HEAT and KE attack using Brenus explosive reactive armour modules. (Giat)

The object of the visit to AMX was to see the new French AMX 30 battle tank, full production of which had just began. At 32.5 tonnes it was the lightest of its generation of battle tanks and it incorporated several unusual features including a 105mm rifled gun which fired the unique Obus G armour-piercing ammunition. This incorporated a shaped charge, mounted on ball bearings to minimise any spin imparted to it by the gun's rifling and consequently avoiding any reduction in its armour penetration.

On the way to the AMX establishment I called, as a matter courtesy, on the British military attaché in Paris who warned me that I might not see much of the AMX 30, as he and other allied attaches were only shown one, briefly, driven past them. However, when on the following day I called on the director of AMX, Monsieur Bodin, we had a friendly discussion after which he told me that an AMX 30 was standing, waiting for me to inspect at leisure! I subsequently wrote, with the assistance of the AMX establishment, a short account of the design and development of the AMX 30 which was published in Britain in the series entitled *AFV Profiles* and subsequently reprinted in a book on "Modern Battle Tanks".

GIAT AMX 10RC reconnaissance vehicles armed with low-pressure 105mm guns in service with the French Army during the 1991 Gulf War. (SIRPA)

I remained in contact with Monsieur Bodin for some time and continued with his successor, Monsieur Viviez, who was to introduce me at the 1971 Satory exhibition to an unusual experimental wheeled armoured vehicle, which was skid-steered like a tracked vehicle and which became the prototype of the AMX 10 RC reconnaissance vehicle produced later for the French Army. My contacts with AMX continued in a less formal way at these biennial French military equipment exhibitions, which were held next to the AMX establishment at Satory. I first attended what was the second of these exhibitions in 1969 - and subsequently every one until 2010. By then what was originally called the Satory Exhibition had become (from 1992), the Eurosatory international exhibition and as such moved in 2000 to the more extensive grounds at Villepinte, north of Paris, while AMX became a part of the GIAT defence industry conglomerate.

Except for AMX 10 RC, AMX was concerned with the design and development of tanks and other tracked armoured vehicles, while private companies produced wheeled armoured vehicles. The most prominent and oldest of these was Panhard & Levassor, which retained this name even after a merger with the Andre Citroen company.

The EBR 75 reconnaissance vehicle developed and produced by Panhard during the 1950s. (Panhard)

Christian Dumont with RMO in 2003, on a visit to the French Musée des Blindés at Saumur. The latter's exhibits include this Stillbrew Chieftain decked out in the urban camouflage pattern first introduced by the British Army's Berlin Brigade in the 1980s.

I was particularly interested in the unconventional features of some of the vehicles designed by Panhard, such as the eight-wheeled EBR (*Engin Blindé de Reconnaissance*) which had four centre, tractor-type wheels that were retracted for road operation and but could be lowered for driving over soft ground. EBR also had an unconventional, 'oscillating' turret consisting of two parts, the upper part of which mounted the vehicle's 75mm gun. The only other French armoured vehicle to be produced with this type of turret has been the widely used AMX 13 light tank.

I visited Panhard for the first time in 1966 when it was producing the four- wheeled AML (*Auto Mitrailleuse Légère*). This vehicle was inspired to some extent by the British Daimler Ferret scout car, some of which were used for a time by the French Army, and weighed only 5.5 tonnes. However, it was armed with a medium-velocity 90mm gun capable of firing anti-tank as well as other projectiles which made it more effective, in relation to its weight, than other contemporary armoured vehicles. In consequence it was produced not only for the French Army but also for 53 other armed forces around the world and its total production reached 4,812 vehicles.

My original visit to Panhard was followed by several others during which I established friendly relations with Francois Bedaux, its managing director. who invited me to his home as well as arranging meetings in Paris and who I entertained when he visited London. When he retired I continued my close contacts with Panhard through one its executives, Christian Dumont, who was also an armoured vehicle historian. Christian joined the company in 1971 after two years of military service in the 501st tank regiment, the French Army's oldest tank regiment which was still equipped at the time with US-built M47 tanks, and I continued my contacts with him even when he retired after 34 years with Panhard.

During the course of my visits to Panhard I was able to study at first hand not only the AML but also vehicles which followed it. The first of them was the ERC 90 (Engin de Reconnaissance a Canon de 90) which was a six-wheeled derivative of the AML but armed with a more powerful 90mm gun and still light enough to be used by the French airborne forces. Next Panhard produced the VBL (*Véhicule Blindé Légère*), a very well designed, turretless, armoured scout vehicle of 3.8 tonnes which began to come into large-scale use with the French Army in 1990.

Before this, Panhard competed unsuccessfully with the SAVIEM company for an order from the French Army for its principal wheeled armoured personnel carrier and also with the Berliet truck company for an armoured carrier for the *Gendarmerie*. While Berliet's VXB 170 armoured carrier was being promoted I was invited twice to the Berliet factory in Lyon to attend demonstrations of its prototype, which was simple but well suited to internal security operations. But eventually only 200 vehicles were ordered for the *Gendarmerie,* and Berliet merged with SAVIEM to form the Renault Trucks company which became responsible for the VAB wheeled armoured personnel carrier selected by the French Army.

Mobility demonstration of Renault's VAB in its 6x6 and 4x4 versions.

The first VAB were produced in 1974 and I was able to view and drive one at the time. As often happens at demonstrations, that of the VAB was interrupted by a minor hiccup, caused by the engine fan belt breaking! But this was quickly rectified and the demonstration was successfully resumed of what proved to be a well proportioned design produced in four and six-wheeled forms. These came to be used on a large scale by the French Army and also by the armed forces of a number of other countries

I did not visit the remaining French company specialising at the time in wheeled armoured vehicles until 2001. That company was ACMAT of Saint Nazaire and the immediate object of the visit to it was to view and comment on the VLRB, a robust, mechanically simple, four-wheeled, turretless armoured carrier which was being offered by ACMAT to the British Army to meet one of its requirements. The offer was not accepted but VLRB proved very successful when used by French and other forces in different parts of Africa, particularly where the terrain was difficult and maintainance facilities were limited.

By then GIAT Industries, which succeeded AMX as the producer of French tanks, entered the field of wheeled armoured vehicles and developed to French Army requirements the eight-wheeled VBCI, or *Véhicule Blindé de Combat d'Infanterie*. Prototypes of it began to be built in 2004 and a year later I went to France to see one of them at GIAT's facilities at Satory and on the following day delivered a lecture there. The French Army subsequently ordered 700 and successfully deployed some for the first time in 2010 on operations in Afghanistan, as mentioned in the previous chapter.

In addition to the producers of armoured vehicles my contacts extended to other companies in the French defence industry.

One of them was Nord Aviation (later Aérospatiale) which, building on the pioneering German attempt to develop an anti-tank guided missile towards the end of the Second World War, produced the Western World's first such missile to become operational, the SS.10. Through its office in London, Aérospatiale kept me informed of the development of its missiles and, in addition to arranging meetings, flew me in 1968 in one of its aircraft from Paris to Bourges, there to see the plant where it produced some of the missiles and in particular the ENTAC anti-tank missile which by then had succeeded the SS.10.

Belgium

My visits to France were interspersed for a time by others to Belgium, to view and to discuss tank-related developments there. Belgium is not generally associated with tanks but it was, in fact, the first country after Germany to order Leopard 1 tanks when these began to be produced, receiving them between 1968 and 1971. Moreover, the Belgian SABCA aerospace company was in the forefront of the development of computerised tank fire control systems and in particular one for the Leopard 1 tank. This fire control system, called Cobelda, was retrofitted not only in those Leopard 1s acquired by Belgium but was also adopted for those produced for Canada and Australia.

SABCA invited me in 1970 to come to Brussels to see and to discuss the tank gun fire control system which they were developing and which, among others, incorporated a laser range finder. Such range finders were still viewed at the time with some scepticism because the early versions would produce, under some conditions, false echoes and therefore incorrect range information. However, laser range finders proved to be superior to the optical range finders hitherto the most advanced means of determining target range, and subsequently I tried to bring out their advantages in my writing and lectures.

I was invited to visit SABCA again in 1977 and 1982, to follow progress in the further development of Cobelda, and eventually in 1991 to attend a demonstration of an upgraded version of it.

A prototype of ACEC's Cobra tracked armoured carrier with electric transmission. (ACEC)

In between, in 1981, I also visited Belgium at the invitation of the Fabrique Nationale (FN), which took me to its armaments factory in Herstal where I saw some of its products, and where I was presented with a scale model of the recently developed FN M240 7.62 mm light machine gun. I was then also taken to ACEC in Charleroi, where I saw the prototype of the Cobra tracked armoured carrier with an electric transmission developed from the basis of the M24 light tank fitted with an experimental form of this type of transmission which I had seen several years earlier.

A spotlessly attired RMO prepares to drive one of the prototype Timoney armoured carriers at the Curragh in 1975. The design was later adopted as the basis of the BDX internal security vehicle manufactured in Belgium by Beherman Demoen. (Timoney)

A reunion between S-tank designer Sven Berge and RMO at the Satory exhibition in France in 1990.

Later that year I went to Belgium again, this time at the invitation of the Beherman Demoen Company of Mechelen. It followed a visit I made six years earlier to Dublin to meet Professor Seamus Timoney and one of his brothers and to see the four-wheeled armoured carrier which they built, in their garage, as a potential competitor to the Panhard AML light armoured cars that were procured at the time by the Irish Army. I drove the Timoney carrier on the Curragh and, although it stood in need of some refinement, I commented favourably on it in an article which I subsequently wrote for *International Defense Review*. This attracted the attention of the Belgian authorities and led to Beherman Demoen receiving an order for 80 BDX derivatives of the Timoney carrier for use by the Gendarmerie as an internal security vehicle and also for airfield security.

Sweden

A few years before I first went to Belgium I started visiting Sweden. My first visit there, in 1964, followed an exchange of letters with Sven Berge who was Chief Engineer of the Mobility Directorate of the Swedish Defence Materiel Administration (FMV) and the designer of the highly original, unconventional, turretless S-tank. Seeing the latter was the main object of my visit and I made it at the invitation of the Bofors company which was developing the tank.

When I met him Sven Berge told me that he originally advanced the concept of the S-tank in 1956, inspired in part by the successful employment by the German Army during the Second World War of the turretless *Sturmgeschutz*, or assault gun. But, unlike the latter, the S-tank was to have its gun fixed in relation to the hull, one consequence of which was that the gun was elevated or depressed by altering the pitch of the hull - which was done by means of an adjustable, hydropneumatic suspension. Another consequence of the gun being fixed in the hull was that it could only be traversed by turning the S-tank by means of the steering system incorporated in its transmission. On the other hand, the fixed gun mounting made possible a relatively simple automatic loading system as there was no relative angular movement between the gun and the ammunition magazine. In this respect the S-tank resembled the automatic loading system in the oscillating turret of the French AMX 13 light tank, which the Swedish Army tested in the 1950s, and it became, after the latter, the second tank in the world to be produced with an automatic loading system.

A 2004 photograph of a late-model S-tank, fitted with frontal bar armour and demountable fuel cans along its sides to give additional protection against hollow-charge attack. Its fixed 105mm gun barrel is being depressed with the aid of the tank's hydropneumatic suspension system. (R.Hilmes)

Another novel feature of the S-tank was that it was the first tank in the world to be powered by a gas turbine, albeit in combination with a diesel engine. Its engine system resembled the "combined diesel and gas", or CODAG, system which was beginning to be adopted at the time in naval shipbuilding and, like the latter, offered the advantage of the fuel efficiency of a diesel for general operation with the high output of a gas turbine provided, for additional power, when required.

The most remarkable feature of the S-tank was that it could be fully operated by one man - the first and still the only tank in the world in which this could be done, due to the integration of its steering and elevation controls with the controls for remotely loading and firing its gun. The controls were incorporated in a box with handle-bars, the twisting of which elevated the gun while rotation of the box about its vertical axis steered the tank and, by turning it, traversed the gun. The control box also contained push buttons for activating the loading and firing of the tank's gun.

In most respects the S-tank was superior to conventional, turretted tanks except for its inability to fire effectively on the move. This did not matter at the time it was being developed when all tanks had to stop to fire accurately, which the S-tank could do as quickly as any of them. But this was no longer the case when stabilised gun controls were improved, allowing accurate fire on the move which the S-tank could not do, unless the target happened to be straight ahead of it.

I saw an S-tank, or Strv 103, for the first time on arrival at Bofors in Karlskoga and it happened to be one of a pre-production batch of ten ordered by the Swedish Army in advance of a full-production order. After two days of discussions I returned to Stockholm, where I met Sven Berge with whom I was able to talk at length about the development of the S-tank, and where I was invited to make a presentation to the Military Technical Society.

I flew to Sweden again in the following year, first to attend a firing demonstration at the Swedish Army Anti-Aircraft School at Väddö, north of Stockholm, of the prototype of the VEAK 40 twin 40mm self-propelled anti-aircraft gun, which was developed as a successor to the 40mm Bofors towed anti-aircraft gun very widely used by British, US and other forces during the Second World War. Apart from its advanced electronics, a feature of VEAK 40 was a chassis powered by a diesel and gas turbine combination, like the S-tank. Back in Stockholm I had more discussions with Sven Berge and the commander of the Swedish Armoured Corps, after which I revisited Bofors where I was able this time to operate an S-tank. I then flew to Örnsköldsvik in middle Sweden at the invitation of the Hägglunds company

which was producing the Pbv 302 tracked, amphibious, armoured carrier, generally similar to the widely used US-built M113 APC but superior to it in having a turret-mounted 20mm cannon and not only an externally mounted machine-gun. After viewing the production of Pbv 302 I was driven in one, along a forest track, at up to 46mph to demonstrate its mobility!

In 1967 I revisited Sweden to attend another demonstration of the S-tank at Bofors, after which I was able to drive it and then visited the Swedish Armour School at Skövde and Sven Berge in Stockholm.

By 1968 the British Army had taken an interest in the S-tank and two were brought to the Royal Armoured Corps Centre at Bovington in Dorset for trials, which I was invited to attend. The Bovington trials were followed by further, larger-scale trials by a British tank regiment stationed in Germany but in the end the British Army decided not to adopt the S-tank. The US Army had also taken an interest in the S-tank and had one brought for trials at the US Army Armor Center at Fort Knox in Kentucky but, like the British Army, eventually decided not to adopt it.

RMO being shown round Hägglunds' 16t Ikv91 amphibious tank destroyer. It was armed with a low-pressure 90mm gun, complemented by two 71mm Lyran flare mortars visible on top of its turret.

In the meantime, in 1969, I was invited to give a lecture at the Swedish Royal Military Academy in Stockholm which involved another visit to Sweden. A year later I flew once again to Sweden to attend a firing demonstration of the Ikv 91, a tracked armoured anti-tank vehicle with a turret-mounted 90mm gun newly built by Hägglunds after which I revisited the Armour School and Bofors. I flew back from Stockholm in a De Havilland Comet which was the world's pioneer jet airliner but the original version of which suffered a number of catastrophic failures. After years of almost annual visits to Sweden I did not make another until 1976 when I was invited to give a lecture at the Armour School. This was followed by delivering a lecture and discussions at Bofors and then a flight to Hägglunds at Örnsköldsvik where I gave another lecture. By then Bofors had completed the production of the 290 S-tanks which the Swedish Army had ordered and, at the instigation of Sven Berge, were exploring in collaboration with Hägglunds the design of different armoured vehicles, lighter than the S-tank but still heavily armed. This culminated in the construction of another innovative experimental vehicle, the UDES XX 20, a tracked, articulated, armoured vehicle consisting of two parts. The front part carried a pedestal-mounted 120mm tank gun and housed a crew of three while the rear part contained the engine and the ammunition.

○
The Bofors/Hägglunds UDES XX 20 test bed. (Bofors)

The adoption of an articulated configuration followed the successful production by Volvo of the Bv 202 articulated, tracked, all-terrain carrier which was better able to operate on very soft ground and in deep snow than conventional tracked vehicles because of its very low ground pressure. As a result of its performance in difficult terrain Bv 202 and its successor, Hägglunds' Bv 206, were acquired by the Swedish Army and by several other armies, world-wide, and production of Bv 206 eventually exceeded 11,000 units.

A test bed version of UDES XX 20 was built in the late 1970s and in 1982 I was invited to a demonstration of it. It lived up to expectation so far as its exceptional obstacle-crossing ability was concerned and it looked promising in other respects. But the problem of loading its gun from a magazine in the rear half of the vehicle had not been solved and further development of it was eventually abandoned.

In the meantime Bofors was focussing its attention on the development of a novel anti-tank guided missile named BILL, or RBS 56. This differed from the predecessor anti-tank missile called "Bantam" and others of its generation, like the pioneer French SS.10, in not being a direct, line-of-sight missile but an overflying, top-attack missile. As such it represented a response to the increases in the frontal protection of contemporary tanks and, in general terms, a considerable potential extension of the anti-tank capabilities of ground forces. In consequence, it attracted considerable interest and to foster it Bofors organized in 1985 a large-scale demonstration at the Swedish Army firing range at Ravlunda in Southern Sweden, which I was invited to attend. The demonstration involved the firing of a BILL missile at a Centurion tank, moving some distance away under remote control. This was hit, setting off the ammunition stowed in it in a spectacular demonstration of the effectiveness of BILL.

Earlier in the same year I was again at Örnsköldsvik where I was invited by Hägglunds to speak at a symposium on light armoured vehicles and then attended a demonstration at the firing range at Tame, near Lulea in northernmost Sweden, where I repeated my symposium lecture. A year later I paid a short visit to Karlskoga to attend briefings on the BILL missile and a year later still I flew to Stockholm. There I met Sven Berge and then proceeded once again to Karlskoga to attend a firing demonstration of the BILL anti-tank missile and of the BAT 90mm recoilless anti-tank gun at the Bofors artillery range.

Three years lapsed before I visited Sweden again, this time to attend the 1992 International Symposium on Ballistics in Stockholm. My wife came with me and we spent a very enjoyable week before the symposium sightseeing in Stockholm and in its area. This included seeing the restoration work being carried out on the 17th century ship *Vasa* recovered from the mud of Stockholm harbour where it had sunk when it was being launched, and the castle and Linnaeus Gardens in Uppsala. After the symposium I was invited to give a lecture in Stockholm to the Military Technical Society.

After Sven Berge retired, I maintained my contacts with armoured vehicle developments in Sweden through Rickard Lindstrom, who was a chief engineer in the Combat Vehicle Division of the Swedish Defence Administration (FMV). I first met Rickard Lindstrom in the late 1980s and like Sven Berge he became a personal friend. In the 1990s he became involved in design studies which led to another innovative Swedish armoured vehicle programme, that of the SEP modular vehicles, for which he was Project Manager and he kept me informed of its progress.

The SEP programme involved the development of relatively light tracked and wheeled armoured carriers which shared many components and incorporated some of the latest advances in armoured vehicle technology. Thus, both versions had double floors which increased protection

The SEP-W (wheeled) 6x6 and SEP-T (tracked) prototypes with electric transmissions. A mechanically driven 8x8 version was later added to the family in the hope of capturing the British Army's FRES Utility Vehicle development and production contract. (BAe Hägglunds)

against the blast of mine explosions and, in the case of the tracked version, also reduced the transmission of track noise which was attenuated from the start by the use of rubber band-tracks instead of the more conventional, metal, link-tracks.

Both versions were powered by a pair of the same make of diesel engine located in the sponsons and coupled to electric transmissions. In addition to their steel armour, they were to be protected by a novel active protection system developed in Germany by IBD Deisenroth Engineering. This incorporated hard kill, explosive counter-measures and proved very effective against RPG-7 rocket propelled grenades when they were fired at one of the SEP vehicles during a demonstration.

The first SEP test vehicle, which was tracked, was completed in 2000 and was followed three years later by a 6x6 wheeled vehicle. It was originally hoped in Sweden that another country might participate in the SEP programme and share in its cost. In fact, in 2006, the British Ministry of Defence began to consider including a SEP in its FRES programme and an 8x8 version with a mechanical driveline instead of the electric drive was consequently built to its requirements. However, it rejected the SEP vehicle a year or so later and,

in the absence of another international partner, the Swedish Army cancelled the programme in 2008.

In the meantime, in 2002, Rickard Lindstrom was appointed Strategic Specialist in Combat Vehicles at FMV and I was invited to the appointment ceremony in Stockholm, to which I contributed a presentation on armoured vehicle development. In the following year I made another visit to Sweden, this time at the invitation of the Hägglunds company to a demonstration in Örnsköldsvik of the vehicles which it was producing at the time: the CV9030, the 30mm cannon-armed export version of the highly successful CV90; the CV9040 infantry fighting vehicle armed with a 40mm Bofors cannon produced for the Swedish Army; and the Bv 206S and BvS 10 armoured articulated tracked carriers. I drove all three of them which proved easy, although the articulated vehicles were slower to respond to steering controls than the more conventional tracked vehicle.

Four years later I made my last visit to Sweden, to attend the All-Electric Combat Vehicles Conference mentioned already in this chapter. As on an earlier occasion, my wife came with me and we enjoyed some more sightseeing in

Test driving the Bv206S armoured articulated carrier (above) and CV9030 infantry combat vehicle (below) during a visit to Hägglunds in June 2003.

Stockholm, including a visit to the beautifully restored *Vasa*, the ship we saw being worked on 15 years earlier, while I attended a presentation of some of the SEP vehicles.

After it cancelled the SEP programme, the Swedish Army ordered in its place a hundred-odd AMVs (Armoured Modular Vehicles) designed by the Finnish Patria company. As it happens, several years before this - in 2004 in fact - I had visited Patria at Hämeenlinna in Finland where I was briefed on the design of the AMV and had one of the first two pre-production vehicles demonstrated to me as well as being shown AMVs being built. At the end of the visit I was driven to the nearby Finnish Tank Museum at Parola where I saw an interesting collection of Soviet tanks captured by the Finnish Army during the Second World War.

AMV was an eight-wheeled armoured carrier and was the first such vehicle to be designed and produced by Patria, whose prior experience was confined to building the simpler armoured carriers taken over from the Sisu company. Nevertheless, it proved to be a sound, well-designed and well-armoured vehicle which gained widespread approval. In consequence, even before it began to be produced, the Polish Ministry of Defence placed an order for 690 vehicles and followed it with another for 307 vehicles, which were produced in Poland under licence as Rosomaks. More were adopted by other countries in Europe and others were also produced under licence by the Denel company in South Africa, as Badgers.

Some years before I went to Finland, I also visited Norway. I was there in 1999 as a result of an invitation to lecture at the Norwegian War Academy (*Krigeskolan*) in Oslo. In addition to two days of lecturing on armoured vehicles I spent some time being shown various sights around Oslo, including the Viking Ship Museum and in it a beautifully preserved 9th century Viking ship, and the Kon-Tiki Museum dedicated to the raft on which Thor Heyerdahl crossed the Pacific in 1947.

Switzerland

Development of armoured vehicles in Switzerland first attracted my attention in 1956 when I learnt of a very unusual, experimental, low-silhouette, tracked weapon carrier, with a two-man crew which operated it in a prone position. This was built in Geneva by the Rexim company. My subsequent contacts with Rexim were confined to correspondence, but I followed the design of its vehicle and found that it was sold to the Fouga company in France, which developed it into the VP 90, a very light two-man turreted tank. The idea of such a vehicle was then taken up by the Hotchkiss company which built a small batch of somewhat more substantial vehicles of this kind as *Engin Légère de Combat* (ELC). These were experimented with by the French Army in the early 1960s but their development was not pursued further.

It was only six years later that I first visited Switzerland and the visit had nothing to do with armoured vehicles. Instead it was related to warships! It resulted from being asked by the Ships Department of the Admiralty to report on a new type of engine piston, developed for large marine diesels by the Sulzer company. This took me to Winterthur where Sulzer was located and where I spent some time studying the piston on which I subsequently produced a report.

In 1966 I visited Switzerland again, but this time as part of a car tour which eventually took me to Austria. I took advantage of it to spend a day, en route, with the Hispano Suiza company in Geneva with which I had been in contact, mainly about its 20mm automatic cannons. Two days later I spent a day with the Mowag Motorwagenfabrik, a privately owned company in Kreuzlingen on Lake Constance, with which I had already corresponded for a couple of years. Mowag had only started to design and build armoured vehicles in 1953, but just six years later received an order for the MR 8 armoured car which was subsequently produced under licence in Germany for the Federal Border Police.

○
Switzerland's first indigenous battle tank, the Pz 61, armed with the British L7 105mm gun and powered by an MTU V-8 diesel engine.

In between the visits to Hispano Suiza and Mowag I spent a day at the Federal Construction Works (K+W) in Thun, which proved to be a very versatile establishment involved in the maintainance and production of a wide range of military equipment, even including aircraft in the past. It was there that I saw the object of my visit, which was to see the new Swiss Pz 61 tank and I was then given the opportunity to drive one. To visit K+W I applied in advance for permission to the Swiss embassy in London which responded initially by asking which British government department would sponsor the visit. As it happens none was involved but, in spite of being informed of this, the Swiss authorities agreed to the visit and when I arrived in Thun I was accorded a very friendly reception and was shown what I wanted to see.

My reason for wanting to see Pz 61 was not only that it was the first tank ever produced in Switzerland but also because it incorporated a number of unusual or novel features. One of them was a hull cast in one piece, which until then had only been done in the United States, for the M48 tank. The production of the hull was a considerable achievement on the part of Swiss foundrymen and eliminated the need to import thick armour plate which was not produced in Switzerland. Pz 61 also incorporated a transmission which was conceptually ahead of others in having hydrostatically controlled steering and it had a unique suspension system with conical plate springs instead of the usual coil springs or torsion bars.

Three years after my first visit to K+W in Thun I was there again, in the course of another car tour, to discuss the development of tanks. Following the visit and correspondence with the Swiss Armament Technology and Procurement Group (GRD) in Bern, I wrote a short history of tank development in Switzerland which was published in Britain in 1972 as part of the *AFV Profiles* series of brochures. Later I had the satisfaction of finding that some of them were being distributed by the GRD as part of its official information pack on Swiss tanks.

In 1975 it was arranged that I should come to Switzerland again, this time to speak in Bern to a gathering of the representatives of the General Staff and the Armoured Corps as well as GRD and K+W, and then to review tank design with members of K+W in Thun. Two years later, I was again invited to come to Switzerland to discuss future tanks with GRD and K+W, in Bern and Thun respectively. The discussions were related, in general terms, to the intention of the Swiss Army to acquire a new tank that would succeed Pz 68, which was a development of the Pz 61 and which was being produced at the time. Contract for the design studies of a new tank was awarded to the Contraves Division of the Oerlikon-Bührle Company which invited me to visit it in 1978 in Zurich and in Geneva.

In the meantime problems had emerged with Pz 68 which raised questions about its continued production. This became a political issue, so much so that the Swiss Parliament set up a committee to examine it. I was invited to appear before it together with a number of others, which I did in July 1979 after calling at K+W where I was briefed on the problems which had been identified. In my opinion the problems which were encountered were not uncommon in newly produced tanks and, provided they were rectified, production of Pz 68 should continue, which it did. My appearance before the committee attracted the attention of the Swiss Press which appeared intrigued by the fact that I was not a Swiss national!

Originally Pz 68 was expected to be followed by a new and much more advanced tank, designated NKPz (*Neuer Kampfpanzer*), which was to be designed by Contraves. The design proved to be sound but Swiss authorities came to the conclusion that Switzerland lacked the infrastructure to develop it into a successful tank, which led to a decision that a new tank would have to be acquired from another country that was already producing tanks. The choice very quickly came down to the German Leopard 2 or the US M1 and specimens of both were subjected to competitive trials in Switzerland between 1981 and 1982. Towards the end of that period I was invited to witness firing trials at a range in the mountains in Eastern Switzerland and then to discuss the relative characteristics of the two competing tanks with GRD in Bern. The discussion brought out, among others, that the fuel consumption of the gas-turbine powered M1 was even worse than I had predicted, and on this as well as other grounds I favoured Leopard 2 being chosen.

In fact, the Swiss Parliament authorised the acquisition of Leopard 2 in 1984. The first 35 came directly from Germany but the rest were assembled, under licence, at K+W. Apart from other considerations, the production of Leopard 2 in Switzerland retained much of its cost within the country and sustained its tank-production facilities and skills, although it did result in a loss of design practice.

Shortly before the decision to produce Leopard 2 in Switzerland as Pz 87, the Swiss Society of Armament Technology (SKG) decided to hold a symposium in 1983 in Zurich and I was invited to speak on tanks and their potential. After this, my next tank-related visit to Switzerland did not take place until 2001 when I attended the 19th International Symposium on Ballistics in Interlaken and met some of the engineers I got to know in connection with Swiss tank development. Later in the same year I took advantage of a holiday in Switzerland to visit, once more, what had been K+W but had since become a part of the RUAG technology company.

The German Leopard 2A4 was produced under licence in Switzerland from 1987, under its Swiss Army designation Pz87. This particular example was used to test the installation of Switzerland's indigenously developed 140mm gun, whose APFSDS sub-projectile could penetrate 1m of steel armour.

During the preceding decade K+W had made considerable progress in several areas which included the development of an experimental, 140mm smoothbore tank gun that was mounted in a Leopard 2. It also developed APFSDS ammunition for the 140mm gun which was capable of penetrating as much as 1,000mm of steel armour.

While the state-run K+W successfully built tanks to their own designs or under licence, the privately owned Mowag company produced wheeled armoured vehicles entirely of its own design. Since I first visited it in 1966, it had designed and built a number of prototypes of tracked as well as wheeled armoured vehicles and I corresponded with as well as meeting Mowag engineers at exhibitions and conferences. But I did not visit the company itself again until 1994. By then Mowag had designed the Piranha family of state-of-the-art, multi-wheeled armoured vehicles and had scored its first major success when, in 1977, it won a Canadian Army competition with a 6x6 version of it. This led to an order for 491 vehicles that were produced under licence by General Motors of Canada. These vehicles in turn served as models for the LAV 25 derivative, in 8x8 configuration, adopted by the US Marine Corps in 1982. These were basically armoured personnel carriers with turret-mounted 25mm automatic cannon, and were followed by other orders for Piranhas, the biggest single order, for 1,117 vehicles, coming from the Saudi Arabian National Guard.

Mowag's Piranha was in fact the forerunner of the wheeled armoured personnel carriers which were adopted almost universally from the 1980s onwards and which started the general use of such features as eight-wheeled running gear with the wheels independently sprung by coil springs, or, in some cases torsion bars, and eventually hydropneumatic springs.

By the time I revisited Kreuzlingen in 1994, Mowag had developed new 6x6 and 10x10 models of the Piranha which I was able to view and to have the opportunity also to drive a prototype of the ten-wheeled vehicle. This, somewhat to my surprise, I found easy to drive and to turn, in spite of its long wheelbase. Two years after this personal visit I was at Mowag again, this time to attend a Press presentation of the re-developed Piranha III vehicle family.

When I visited Kreuzlingen again, in 2005, Mowag had ceased to be an independent, privately owned company, having been sold in 2003 to the US General Dynamics company, as was General Motors of Canada which produced many Piranhas under licence. Moreover, in 2001, what was then still General Motors of Canada received an order from the US Army for 2,131 units, which were basically Canadian (LAV III) versions of the uprated Piranha III 8x8 design. The model ordered by the US Army was intended for its Future Combat Systems (FCS) programme to fulfil its so-called Interim Armoured Vehicle (IAV) requirement and was re-named Stryker.

As a result of all this Mowag was changing in many ways, but I was accorded as friendly a reception as before and was fully briefed on the latest versions of the Piranha. This also applied to my last visit to Kreuzlingen in 2010. In the meantime development of Piranha continued and the total number in use around the world has been estimated at about 9,000. An interesting feature of their production has been that, although most of them were not built in Switzerland, their critical driveline mechanical components were all made in Kreuzlingen.

A year before my last visit to Mowag I went to see the Swiss Military Museum in Full, on the German border. This proved to be a very interesting, privately owned museum containing many different armoured vehicles, including a collection of prototypes and other vehicles built over the years by Mowag which were fortunately bequeathed to the museum when the ownership of the company changed, instead of being scrapped as often happens to historically valuable vehicles on such occasions.

Spain

In between my other visits I also made one in 1976 to Spain where I was invited to lecture on tank technology and recent developments in tank design at the Politecnic University in Madrid. I took advantage of the visit to tour some of the principal sights in Madrid, ranging from the Plaza Mayor in the centre of old Madrid, to the paintings at the Prado Museum. I also visited the monumental Memorial to the Fallen of the Spanish Civil War of the 1930s, carved out of the Guadarama mountains, and the Escorial royal monastery.

Italy

Although my first book on armoured vehicles entitled "Armour: The Development of Armoured Forces and Their Equipment" was translated into Italian at the instigation of the Inspector of the Armoured Troops of the Italian Army and was published in Rome in 1964, I was not involved with Italian armoured vehicles until 1982. I was then approached by the Defence Coordination and Development department of the Fiat company in Turin, which invited me to examine what opportunities there were around the world for retrofitting existing armoured vehicles with more modern components, including Fiat engines. Almost immediately after I produced my report on this I received another invitation, this time to examine the concepts of a multi-purpose six-wheeled armoured vehicle and, shortly afterwards, of a very light four-wheeled armoured carrier.

In 1983 attention became focussed on the four-wheeled version, and I carried out estimates of the weight it might have had using alternative types of armour and of the cost of its different versions as well as producing drawings of how they might have looked, all of which I submitted to Fiat. A year later the studies were followed by the design of an actual vehicle with very similar general characteristics, which was carried out by IVECO-Fiat in Bolzano. It came to be called Puma and a prototype of it was built in 1988. It was subsequently adopted and produced for the Italian Army, not only in its 4x4 form but also as a somewhat larger six-wheeled vehicle.

An Iveco-Fiat Puma 4x4 armoured carrier, whose design drew on studies RMO had undertaken for Fiat in the early 1980s.

Puma was envisaged to be a lightweight armoured personnel carrier which would complement the Centauro, an eight-wheeled vehicle with a turret- mounted 105mm tank gun that was being developed at about the same time by the Consorzio IVECO Fiat - Oto Melara. The two vehicles formed part of an armoured vehicle development programme on which the Italian Army embarked in the early 1980s. Because of its operational mobility, Centauro was considered particularly relevant to the defence of Italy's very long coast line which could not be guarded by stationing troops along the entire length of it, whereas Centauros could move rapidly via the *autostrada* to the threatened sector, much more rapidly than any tracked armoured vehicles could do.

The tracked vehicles also part of the Italian Army's armoured vehicle development programme consisted of the Dardo infantry fighting vehicle (IFV) and the Ariete battle tank. Their primary area of deployment was considered to be the north east of Italy which formed the traditional invasion route. The two tracked and the wheeled armoured vehicles developed and produced for the Italian Army constituted a uniquely comprehensive and coherent acquisition programme, the like of which was not adopted by any other Western army.

In 1989 my contacts with Fiat advanced beyond correspondence and meetings in London or at conferences, when I extended a visit to Krauss Maffei in Munich to proceed to IVECO-Fiat in Bolzano and then on to Oto Melara in La Spezia. At about the same time I applied for permission to see the Ariete battle tank which was then being developed and, as this was granted, I travelled again, a year later, to La Spezia. There, at the beginning of my visit, I saw a VCC-80 which was, in effect, a prototype of the Dardo IFV, except that it was not fitted with a 25mm cannon turret. I was able to drive it on the Oto Melara test ground and found it exceptionally easy so to do. I also found it well designed in general.

Later in the day I saw what was a pre-production version of the Ariete which I also found to be well designed and, on the basis of what I saw, well up to the standard of the contemporary battle tanks. However I was disappointed that it still incorporated electro-hydraulic turret controls which had been commonly used but which were being superceded by safer all-electric controls. I expressed my comments on this after the visit and they were passed on to the Italian authorities. On the other hand I was very pleasantly surprised by the ease with which I was able to get into and out of the driver's station, in contrast to some other tanks in which one had to be, almost, a contortionist.

Two years later, acting as a consultant to General Dynamics Land Systems, I arranged and took part in a visit to IVECO in Bolzano by the chief scientist of GDLS. The company was interested in the Centauro as a result of the US Army's quest for an IAV for its FCS programme. Sixteen Centauros were in fact subsequently leased by the US Army and were tested between 2001 and 2002 but they were not adopted, partly because they were too heavy to meet the somewhat unrealistic air-transportability requirements prescribed for the FCS.

I visited IVECO in Bolzano and Oto Melara in 1996 and 2005 to keep up with the development of the vehicles produced by the two companies. In between I also had meetings in Britain, at demonstrations and conferences, with Maurizio Fazi, the General Manager of IVECO, and with others. I also regularly visited the IVECO stand at the Eurosatory exhibitions where the full range of IVECO and Oto Melara vehicles was on show and during this period I also produced for IVECO and for Oto Melara further studies and reports.

My wife accompanied me on my visits to Bolzano and to La Spezia, and we took advantage of them to see the Leaning Tower of Pisa and to visit the old town of Lucca, as well as sailing along the picturesque coast of the Cinque Terre. On the other occasion we stayed at Lerici on the Bay of the Poets, where the English poet Shelley was drowned.

Austria

Only one West European country other than those already mentioned produced a tank of its own design, that country being Austria.

The tank was the SK-105, or Kürassier, a 17.7 tonne light tank or "tank destroyer", armed with a 105mm gun similar to that of the contemporary French AMX 30 battle tank. The gun was mounted in an oscillating turret, based on that of the French AMX 13 light tank, which incorporated a bustle magazine with 12 rounds that were fed automatically into the gun. The tank's chassis was based on that of a much modified low-silhouette tracked armoured infantry carrier which was developed by Saurer from 1956.

Development of SK-105 was begun by Saurer in Vienna ten years later, but in 1970 was taken over by the Steyr-Daimler-Puch company, also in Vienna, which began its production in 1972. Until 1988 Austria was not allowed, by the peace treaty imposed on it after the Second World War, to have anti-tank guided missiles, and SK-105 with its 105mm tank gun was envisaged to fill the resulting gap in the Austrian Army's anti-tank capabilities. The SK-105 continued to be used into the 2000s, by which time more than 600 had been produced, with recovery and other support-vehicle versions in addition, not only for the Austrian Army but also for armies of countries as far afield as Argentina, Bolivia and Botswana as well as Morocco and Tunisia and even for the Marines of the Brazilian Navy.

The successful production of SK-105 led to further development of it, focussed on increasing its anti-tank capabilities by re-arming it with a higher-pressure 105mm tank gun of the L7 type then still widely used in battle tanks. This involved Rheinmetall which was prompted to develop a low recoil-force version of the L7 by fitting it with a muzzle brake and allowing much longer recoil. In consequence the resulting Rh 105-11 gun could be fired from vehicles much lighter than the tanks in which the L7 gun had previously been mounted. The outcome of it was a new A3 version of SK-105 armed with a low recoil-force 105mm tank gun, but only one experimental model of it was built, in 1988.

However, Rheinmetall's lead was followed in several countries by the installation of low recoil-force 105mm tank guns on vehicles considerably lighter than battle tanks, as already mentioned earlier in this chapter. Among them were the US M8 Armored Gun System and, ultimately, the US M1128 Mobile Gun System based on the eight-wheeled chassis of the Stryker family of vehicles.

The US Army's M8 Armored Gun System, armed with an M35 lightweight 105mm gun, was type classified in 1997 but then shelved.

The US Army eventually fulfilled its Mobile Gun System (MGS) requirement with the M1128, a variant of its Stryker vehicle family derived from Mowag's original 8x8 Piranha III design built by GD in Canada as the LAV III. The MGS has an M68A1E4 105mm rifled gun fitted with a muzzle brake and autoloader.

I first saw an SK-105 in 1981 after meeting the Managing Director of Steyr-Daimler-Puch, Dr. Franz Felberbauer, at a symposium of the Defence Manufacturers Association in Brighton, who invited me to visit his company. I did this a few months later when I visited the Steyr works in Vienna and not only saw an SK-105 but also had an opportunity of driving it. I found this easy compared with a number of other tracked armoured vehicles because of its unique, hydrostatically driven steering mechanism incorporated in the modified version of the Saurer tracked carrier chassis.

By the time I visited Vienna again in 1985, Steyr had embarked on their own initiative on the development of a six-wheeled armoured carrier which came to be called Pandur, after the 18th century Austrian frontiersmen. I was impressed with its automotive design and in particular with its drive-line and independent suspension. As I was in close contact at the time with Royal Ordnance, I suggested that it built Pandur under licence and offered it to the British Army which was in need of wheeled armoured carriers for its infantry. However, as already mentioned in the previous chapter, the UK Ministry of Defence opted instead for Saxon, a cheaper, four-wheeled armoured truck which I described in my contemporary correspondence as "an insult to the British Army".

GKN's Saxon: "an insult to the British Army." (UK MoD)

One of the potential users of the Pandur was Kuwait and a couple of prototypes of it were sent there for demonstration purposes, only to be lost when Saddam Hussein invaded Kuwait in 1990. Production of the Pandur only began after my next visit to Vienna, in 1993, when I called on Steyr to bring myself up to date on the progress the company was making. Initially Pandur was built for Kuwait and the Austrian Army but later it was also built for Slovenia and in a stretched 8x8 form for Portugal and the Czech Republic.

In the 1980s Steyr also began to study the design of a tracked infantry fighting vehicle, but found it could not finance its development by itself. In consequence, it joined forces with the Spanish Santa Barbara company which led in 1988 to the formation of the Austro-Spanish Cooperation Development, or ASCOD, consortium. This resulted in 1991 in the construction of a jointly developed prototype which I saw the following year, at the 1992 Eurosatory exhibition.

The ASCOD infantry combat vehicle armed with a Mauser MK30 cannon, which formed the basis of the Spanish Army's Pizarro and Austrian Army's Ulan vehicles.

Production of the Spanish version, which was called Pizarro, followed in 1996 and eventually amounted to 261 vehicles, while that of the Austrian version, called Ulan or Lancer, began in 1999 and came to 112 vehicles. However, in 2003 Santa Barbara and Steyr as well as the Swiss Mowag company were all bought out by General Dynamics in the US. This ultimately led to a third version of the ASCOD vehicle, built by the newly formed General Dynamics UK company which in 2014 received an order for it from the British Ministry of Defence. Called Ajax, it turned out to be 10 tonnes heavier than the Austrian and Spanish versions and was not armed, as they were, with a 30mm Mauser automatic gun but with the newly developed Anglo-French 40mm externally (electrically) powered CTA cannon which fired case-telescoped ammunition. In its turreted version, Ajax also differed from the earlier vehicles in having a crew of only three whereas they could accommodate, in addition, up to eight infantrymen.

GD's uprated ASCOD 2 design provided the basis for the British Army's Ajax vehicle family, seen here in its reconnaissance variant which has a crew of three and a turret fitted with a 40mm CTA cannon firing case-telescoped ammunition.

In the meantime Dr. Felberbauer had left Steyr for the Austrian Ministry of Defence, but I kept in touch with him and instigated his participation in the 1992 Armoured Warfare Conference in London as well as visiting him and the Steyr company in Vienna in the following year. My wife accompanied me on this occasion and we enjoyed visiting various museums, art galleries and other sights in Vienna. Dr. Felberbauer very kindly drove us along the Danube to see the ruins of the Dürnstein castle (where in the 12th century King Richard the Lionheart was imprisoned when he was returning to England from a crusade), after which we visited the famous 18th century baroque monastery at Melk. Dr. Felberbauer also translated into German my book "Technology of Tanks" and arranged for it to be published in three parts in 1998 and 1999 as "Technologie der Panzer" in the *Truppendienst* series of publications of the Austrian Ministry of Defence.

I made one more visit to Vienna, in 1998, to deliver a course of lectures on armoured vehicles at the General Staff College. As before, I took advantage of the opportunity to revisit Steyr to bring myself up to date on its activities.

Chapter 4
Tank studies and lectures in the United States

My writing on armoured vehicles attracted the attention of the US Army Research Office in Durham, North Carolina, which invited me in 1961 to visit the United States to lecture on them at the principal US Army and defence industry establishments.

The third pilot model of the M60E1, a precursor to the improved M60A1 tank with a 105mm rifled gun in a revised turret, that first ran in June 1961. (US Army)

The US Air Force C-118A, a military version of the Douglas DC-6 airliner, the type of transport on which RMO made his first official trip to America in 1961. (USAF)

In contrast to my first, private visit by sea to the United States 11 years earlier, I flew instead of sailing, this time aboard a piston-engined, propeller-driven Douglas DC-6 aircraft of the US Military Air Transport Service. The visit lasted about a month and involved lecturing on the contemporary state of the development, world-wide, of tanks and other armoured vehicles and on possible further developments of them and their components at eight different military and industrial establishments. They included the Pentagon in Washington, Frankford Arsenal in Philadelphia, Ballistics Research Laboratory at the Aberdeen Proving Ground in Maryland and the US Army Armor Centre at Fort Knox in Kentucky. At Fort Knox I was given an opportunity to drive an M60 tank and to "swim" an M113 amphibious armoured carrier in an adjoining lake, both of which were beginning to come into service at the time. In both cases all went well, but as the M113 was driven out of the water I realized that it was watched at a distance by a motor boat and that there was also a recovery vehicle and an ambulance positioned discretely on the edge of the lake: the Armor Center was obviously prepared for all eventualities!

I then went on to lecture at the Ordnance Tank-Automotive Command in Detroit and at the defence divisions there of the three major US automotive companies - Chrysler, Ford

Original version of the US Army's aluminium-armoured M113 carrier, with its splashboard deployed for amphibious operations. (US Army)

and General Motors. Subsequently the US Army Research Office printed and circulated copies of the lectures.

Shortly after my lecture tour of the United States the US Army Research Office also invited me to take part in the "First International Conference on the Mechanics of Soil-Vehicle Systems", sponsored by the US and Italian armies at the Turin Technical University. The object of the Conference was to promote a better scientific understanding of the problem of operating vehicles in different types of terrain and in particular on difficult, soft soils, exemplified in the extreme by the mud and the deep snow encountered on the Russian front during the Second World War. An outcome of the subsequent studies and trials was the production of articulated off-road vehicles which were indeed better adapted to operation on soft soils and snow than conventional vehicles. The prime examples of them have been the articulated tracked carriers produced in Sweden, first by Volvo and then the Hägglunds company and adopted by many Western armies from the 1970s onwards.

I had already written articles on soil-vehicle mechanics and on articulated vehicles in *THE ENGINEER* and, after taking part in the Turin conference, I became a founder member of the International Society for Vehicle-Soil Systems (ISTVS). I also arranged the publication in Britain of the inaugural issue of its journal. However, I found that I could not combine the study of soil-vehicle mechanics with my other activities and after a time abandoned pursuing it, although I retained an interest in the subject.

In 1967 I made another visit to the United States, making a further advance in my mode of travel by flying in a Vickers VC-10 jet airliner. The principal object of the visit was to attend a composite materials conference in Philadelphia and to see the work on plastics materials at Picatinny Arsenal in Dover, New Jersey, as well as the Du Pont company in Wilmington, Delaware. While in Philadelphia I met Frank Piasecki, the US helicopter pioneer, who was working at the time on the development of hovercraft, or air cushion vehicles (ACV), for military purposes and who allowed me to sit at the controls of one of his machines. ACVs were considered at the time to have considerable general military potential as, in contrast to all other types of vehicles, they could go over the softest types of terrain, such as the paddy fields in Vietnam where US forces were operating. However, they proved incapable of going over even relatively low obstacles and consequently their military use proved to be limited to amphibious landing operations.

From the East Coast I flew to California, principally to visit FMC Corporation in San Jose which had developed and was producing the M113 armoured personnel carrier, a very early version of which I had had the opportunity of driving during my visit to Fort Knox five years earlier. I had already established friendly contacts with FMC through correspondence, and the visit extended them to personal contacts which were to last for several years. They included not only further visits to San Jose but also meetings in London with the Vice President of the Ordnance Division of FMC, who became a personal friend, as well as other executives when they were visiting Europe.

The M113 carrier was the first armoured vehicle in the world to be produced in quantity using aluminium instead of steel armour and it was amphibious - at least to the extent that it could swim in calm inland waters, as was demonstrated to me five years earlier at Fort Knox. It was also produced in greater number than any other armoured vehicle built in the Western World. In fact, its total production reached about 74,000 vehicles. The principal reason for its large-scale production and world-wide use was its low cost, which was quoted originally to be as low as US $22,000, excluding radio and weapons - in 1960 dollars, of course!

I took advantage of my visit to California to tour San Francisco and to visit an old friend in Santa Barbara, Dr. M.G. Bekker, the soil-vehicle mechanics expert, who was working at the time at the AC Defense Research Laboratories on unconventional, articulated vehicles that could be operated on what were considered to be lunar soils, as part of the contemporary moon-landing programme. From there I flew east to take part in the Armor Association annual meeting at Fort Myers, Virginia.

A year later I was in the United States again, primarily to attend and to speak at the centenary conference of the Society of Plastics Engineers in New York. But I took advantage of it to visit Washington, DC, where I had a meeting with Major General E.H. Burba, who was Project Manager of the MBT-70 main battle tank programme which was being pursued at the time by the United States in collaboration with Germany. From Washington I flew to Detroit where I delivered a lecture at the Detroit Arsenal and on the following day visited Chrysler Ordnance in Detroit and its Canadian branch in Windsor, Ontario.

MBT-70 was to be the most advanced battle tank of its day. In fact, it incorporated a number of advanced systems and unusual features, such as the location of all three of its crew in the turret which required the provision of a counter-rotating mini-turret for the driver, so that he faced forward irrespective of the position of the main turret. But several of the new systems and features were untried and called for further development which, inevitably, implied considerable expenditure of effort and money. Moreover, a number of major components, such as engines, transmissions and suspensions, were being developed on a competitive basis in the United States and Germany which implied a duplication of effort and additional costs. Management of the project was also complicated, not least by the existence of separate design offices in the United States and in Germany, the efforts of which had to be harmonized. In consequence the cost of the joint project rose rapidly from the original and very optimistic estimate of US $80 million in 1963 to US $400 million in 1969, by which time it drew the attention of the US Congress. The latter then began to investigate the management of the MBT-70 programme and eventually forced the US Army to abandon it in 1970 as too costly, Germany having already withdrawn from it. I followed the project with very considerable interest and my critical view of it eventually prompted me to write an article entitled "The MBT-70 or How Not to Design a Modern Weapon", which was published in 1970 [in the US engineering publication *Machine Design*].

Honorary Life Membership

My various activities, including contributing many articles to the journal *ARMOR*, led to my being awarded in 1970 an honorary life membership of the US Armor Association. I was only the eighth person to be so honoured in the 84 years of the Association, which was a continuation of the US Cavalry Association, and the only non-US citizen among them. The award was made at a reception in London by Major General M.G. Roseborough, who flew in for the event from Germany where he commanded the 3rd US Armored Division

Two years later I was invited by the Ordnance Systems and Technology Section of the Battelle Memorial Institute of Columbus, Ohio to participate in a study commissioned by the US Defense Advanced Research Projects Agency (DARPA) of the relative effectiveness of different tank and anti-tank weapons against potential enemy tanks. The study was carried out against the background of the decision taken in 1970 by the US Congress to terminate the development of MBT-70, which had been started at a time when the US Army still favoured guided missiles with shaped-charge warheads as tank armament and ended when opinion began to shift in favour of return to guns firing high-velocity projectiles. Having considered a range of the alternatives, the Battelle study in which I participated came to the conclusion that guns firing high-velocity projectiles with long-rod, arrow-like penetrators which had begun to be developed would be the most effective weapons against enemy tanks, as already mentioned in Chapter 2.

The study involved four visits to Columbus, two lasting a month each, and was completed by the end of 1972. Oddly enough, I was not allowed to see the final version of the report on it, even though I had a US SECRET security clearance and actually drafted much of the text of the study. Moreover, when the study was submitted to DARPA it drew the comment from the latter that too much of it appeared to reflect my views!

Battelle Columbus Laboratories asked for my assistance again in 1975. In the interim the 1973 Arab-Israeli Yom Kippur War had taken place, when the initial assault crossing of the Suez Canal by the Egyptian forces was followed by a hasty counter-attack on the part of Israeli tank units, which suffered heavy losses from Soviet-made Sagger anti-tank guided missiles employed by the Egyptian infantry. This immediately led to world-wide claims that "time was running out for the tank", to quote a contemporary article in *The Times*. In response I had to point out repeatedly that tanks were never invulnerable and that many more had been destroyed in the Yom Kippur War by the guns of the opposing tanks than by guided missiles. As a follow up I was invited in 1974 to present a paper on "The future of the battle tank" at a special conference held at Tufts University in Massachusetts, the proceedings of which were published by the University in a book entitled "The other arms race".

The second spell of work at Battelle originated with a US Army decision to create at its Tank-Automotive Command in Detroit a contractor-operated Advanced Concepts Laboratory (ACL) which, it was hoped, would inject new ideas into the whole field of armoured vehicle design and development. Battelle decided to bid for it and I helped to write the proposal which was accepted in 1976. I then acted as a consultant to the ACL, writing a number of studies for it during visits to Detroit and in London over the following three years, concerning different types of armoured vehicles and their technology. But what effect they might have had on US armoured vehicle development I never found out!

The Soviet 9M14 Malyutka (NATO reporting title AT-3 Sagger) manportable anti-tank missile. Its successful use by the Egyptians during the Yom Kippur War precipitated a round of predictions concerning the impending demise of the tank.

AAI's 16-20t High Survivability Test Vehicle – Lightweight (HSTV-L), armed with the Ares XM274 75mm automatic cannon, was the experimental light tank element of DARPA's HIMAG research programme. (AAI)

Before the ACL came into being I was also invited to join an advisory group set up by BDM Corporation, of Vienna, Virginia, which was awarded a contract to review periodically a new DARPA High Mobility-Agility (HIMAG) programme aimed at the construction of a light armoured vehicle armed with a novel, high-velocity, automatically loaded 75mm Ares gun firing what was then the newly developed APFSDS ammunition, considered to be a potential alternative to the contemporary tanks armed with conventional, larger-calibre guns firing the earlier, less effective (APDS) types of armour-piercing ammunition. The Ares gun also had an unconventional, rotary breech and fired case-telescoped ammunition which facilitated automatic loading.

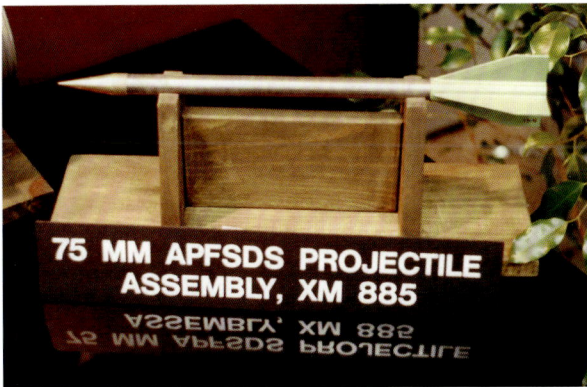

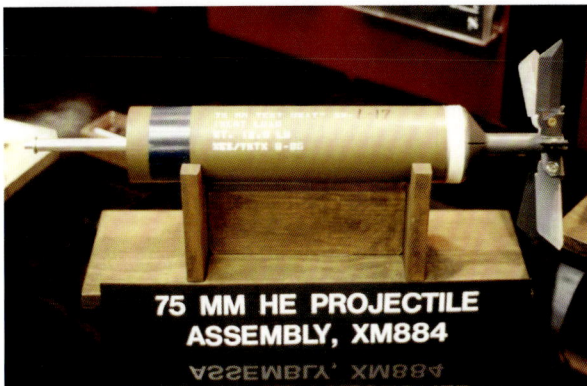

Case-telescoped ammunition, including (top) the XM885 APFSDS and (bottom) XM884 HE rounds, was developed by AAI for the Ares 75mm smoothbore cannon, which had a nominal burst rate of fire of three rounds in 4.5 seconds. (R Pengelley)

At first the HIMAG programme also included an attempt to revive the use of liquid propellants which had been tried before but without success. The revival was prompted by the development by the US Navy of new liquid monopropellants for torpedoes, but was abandoned after it led to a number of uncontrollable explosions and further development reverted to the use of more conventional, solid propellants. The concept of a light tank armed with the 75mm Ares gun

was pursued until 1981 but by then it was overtaken by the development of low-recoil force versions of the existing, 105mm tank guns, pioneered in Germany by Rheinmetall, which could be mounted in relatively light tanks. Moreover, a strong case had already emerged for using tank guns that were larger still in calibre. Thus, during a meeting and in correspondence in 1976 with Norman Augustine, the US Under Secretary of the Army, I argued in favour of arming tanks with 120mm guns, although at the time the US Army was still content to arm the new XM1 tank it was developing with the widely used 105mm rifled gun, albeit made more effective by being provided with APFSDS ammunition which could be fired from it because of the development of slipping driving bands. The latter prevented APDSFS projectiles from being spun by the rifling of the 105mm gun and consequently becoming unstable in flight.

The HIMAG programme was also intended to explore whether high power-to-weight vehicle ratios, and therefore an ability to accelerate rapidly and to execute evasive manoeuvres, such as zig-zagging, could reduce significantly the chances of tanks being hit and therefore improve their survivability. To this end an M60-type tank chassis was fitted with an over-size engine so that its power-to-weight ratio and hence its acceleration could be varied. However no clear conclusion emerged from the tests and the analysis of them.

Although the HIMAG programme was initiated by DARPA, it was pursued in collaboration with the US Army and the US Marine Corps under the title of the Armored Combat Vehicle (ACV) programme and led to the construction of an experimental light tank with the 75mm Ares gun as well as the test bed vehicle whose power-to-weight ratio could be varied. But, by the early 1980s the US Army lost interest in the 75mm Ares gun and its ammunition system. The US Marine Corps retained its interest in the gun a little longer as it appeared to fit its requirement for a Mobile Protected Weapon System. This led to a two-day meeting convened in Washington in February 1981 by the Marine Corps Development Center to review the requirements of the Corps in which I was invited to participate. The outcome of this and other investigations was the rejection of the Ares gun and the adoption by the US Marine Corps of an eight-wheeled Light Armored Vehicle (LAV), armed with a 25mm automatic cannon, which was based on the Piranha I designed in Switzerland by the Mowag company and which was produced under licence in Canada by General Motors.

The HIMAG programme involved attending meetings in Washington and the ACL programme required working in Detroit, which meant that I had to fly several times each year to the United States - six in fact in 1976. When the ACV and HIMAG programmes came to an end, I continued to visit the United States at least once each year. Thus, in the summer of 1980 I spent almost three weeks in the United States, starting with a visit to Muskegon, Wisconsin, to see Teledyne Continental Motors. The company, to whom I was a consultant for a time, was the manufacturer of AVDS-1790 V-12 air-cooled diesel engines for the US M60 and several other tanks. I then flew to Los Angeles in California to visit the Hughes Aircraft Company, which was then in the forefront of the development of tank fire control systems, and drove on from there to Santa Barbara to revisit Dr. M.G. Bekker, the soil-vehicle mechanics expert. I then took advantage of the opportunity to drive along the scenic Highway 1 coastal road to revisit FMC Corporation in San Jose, where on two consecutive days I led discussions of armoured vehicle development. From San Jose I went to lecture at the US Naval Postgraduate School in Monterey and then flew from San Francisco to Louisville, Kentucky to visit, once again, the US Army Armor Centre at Fort Knox. There, prior to attending a dinner held in my honour, I was able to drive an M3 Cavalry Fighting Vehicle counterpart to the newly developed M2 Bradley Infantry Fighting Vehicle and to inspect an XM1 tank which had just been approved for production and service. I then flew back to London via Washington DC, where I paid a short visit to BDM Corporation.

○
RMO in discussion with a member of the US Army during an inspection of the initial 105mm-armed version of the M1 Abrams tank at Ft.Knox

In 1981 I was invited to conduct a two-day colloquium on current trends in armoured fighting vehicles at the US Army Materiel Systems Analysis Activity at the Aberdeen Proving Ground in Maryland. In the following year I lectured again at the Tank Automotive Command in Detroit, as I did in 1983 when I conducted a symposium on the use of test beds in the development of combat vehicles, which became the subject of a technical report published by TACOM.

In 1984 I received an invitation to give the keynote speech at a symposium on "Combat Vehicle Signatures" held at Keweenaw Research Centre of Michigan Technological University at Houghton, Michigan. On the way from it I stopped at Fort Knox, where I was invited by the

Commandant of the US Armor School to talk to the students. Then, on the way back to London, I called once again at TACOM in Detroit.

○
The hull of the experimental composite Bradley M2 infantry fighting vehicle made of S-2 glass-fibre laminate. This gave the same ballistic protection as aluminium armour for a 27 per cent saving in weight. (FMC)

Nine years after my previous visit there, I flew again to California to see the Hughes Aircraft Company in Los Angeles and the FMC Corporation in San Jose, the visit to the latter being combined with attendance at the Armor Conference which was held at the US Naval Postgraduate School in Monterey. During the visit to FMC I was able to examine an experimental version of the M2 Bradley Infantry Fighting Vehicle which had just been built with a hull of glass-fibre plastics instead of aluminium armour. This represented the latest development in light armoured vehicle construction and offered a reduction in weight compared with metallic armours as well some other advantages. But it also involved more elaborate production processes as well as higher costs. So the Bradley vehicle became something of a curiosity as did its British equivalent, built somewhat later, the Advanced Composite Armoured Vehicle Platform or ACAVP, commonly known as the "plastic tank", which was promoted by the Defence Evaluation and Research Agency (DERA) of the Ministry of Defence.

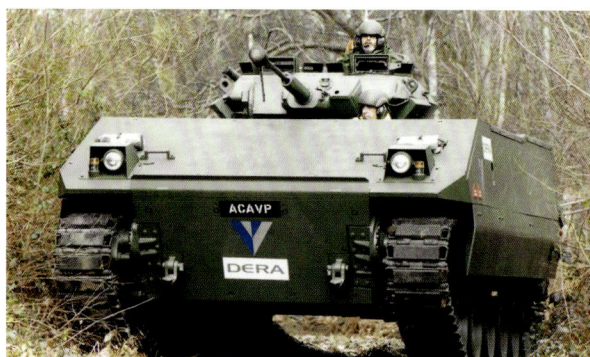

○
The UK's ACAVP composite-hulled demonstration vehicle, constructed of E-glass laminate in the late 1990s, incorporated the automotive systems of the Warrior ICV and a 30mm turret removed from a Fox reconnaissance vehicle. (DERA)

In 1992 I visited Fort Knox again, to speak at the Combat Vehicle Conference of the American Defense Preparedness Association. A new venue presented itself in 1998 when I was invited to run a short course on the technology of tanks and other armoured vehicles at the Institute for Advanced Technology of the University of Texas at Austin. As my host institute was in the forefront of research into electromagnetic guns, lecturing there provided a welcome opportunity to see some aspects of that research at first hand. In the meantime, from 1986 to 1994, I also acted as a consultant to Rand Corporation, the principal US defence think tank. As such I produced for it, from London, a series of papers on the international collaboration in the production of combat vehicles as well as on their development.

Tank engines

Concurrently with the work for Rand I acted as a consultant to General Dynamics Land Systems (GDLS), the producer of the US M1 Abrams tank, having been invited in 1988 to join their Technical Advisory Group (TAG). I already had several years of less formal contacts with GDLS, related mainly to the development of the original XM1 version of the Abrams tank for the US Army. This followed the decision of the US Army to abandon the ill-fated MBT-70 programme, and its short-lived XM803 follow-on, and to issue in 1973 contracts to Chrysler and General Motors for the development of a new and less costly tank. This competition Chrysler won in 1976, its tank being powered by an Avco-Lycoming AGT-1500 gas turbine (derived from a helicopter engine) which was originally intended to be used in MBT-70 but never tried in it. I opposed the adoption of the gas turbine, although the Teledyne AVCR-1360 variable compression-ratio diesel, which had been used in MBT-70 and which General Motors intended to use again in their version of the XM1, was not a better proposition, mainly because of its inconsistent combustion. In fact, its combustion was so erratic that it is said to have produced so much black smoke on one occasion when an MBT-70 was being started that the local fire brigade turned up expecting to find a major fire!

The Avco-Lycoming AGT-1500 1,500hp gas turbine engine, adopted for the US Army's Abrams tank, proved to have a much higher fuel consumption than equivalent diesel engines.

I had written about the possible use of gas turbines to power tanks in an article published in *ARMOR* magazine as early as 1952, when none had yet been installed in any of them, but I qualified my comments with a warning about their possible high fuel consumption. My reservations were brought out when gas turbines began to be tested in tanks and I opposed their adoption for the US XM1 and other tanks mainly because of their significantly higher fuel consumption. However, my views were challenged in my correspondence with the engineering vice president of Chrysler Defense, the company responsible for the development of the XM1 before it was taken over by General Dynamics, who considered the fuel consumption of the gas turbine-powered tank to be acceptable. As part of the debate I wrote a long article on the relative fuel consumption of diesel and gas turbine-powered tanks which was published in the June 1978 issue of *International Defense Review* and in which I estimated that the latter would consume 60 to 70 percent more fuel.

An M1A2 Abrams tank manned by a Swedish Army crew which participated in a 'shoot-off' against the diesel-driven Leopard 2A5 tank in Sweden in March 1993. (CF Foss)

In fact, the situation proved to be even worse, as was demonstrated in the early 1990s when a gas turbine-powered M1A2 tank competed, unsuccessfully, with the diesel-powered German Leopard 2A5 tank for a Swedish Army order: over the same extensive test mileage it used twice as much fuel (just as a preceding model had done during competitive trials in Switzerland in the early 1980s). The gas turbine was also more expensive to produce and the greater fuel consumption of tanks powered by it created a considerable logistics drag on the operational mobility of armoured units. Nevertheless, the gas turbine-powered M1 tank was approved for production by the US Army in 1979. I also raised, through my contacts at the Pentagon, the question of the possibility of serious damage to the AGT-1500 gas turbine adopted for the M1 tank by a mine exploding under it, which would shake the gas turbine while its rotors were spinning at up to 22,500 revolutions per minute. My question led to tests but they showed that the danger was not as serious as was feared.

Dr Philip W. Lett, a General Dynamics VP, was instrumental in the development of both the US Abrams and South Korean K1/K1A1 tanks.
He is seen here with the chief design engineer of Mitsubishi's tank division, Iwao Hayashi (right), and Mrs Hayashi (left).

TAG was set up to discuss world-wide trends in the development of tanks and their impact on new designs. To broaden the discussions it consisted not only of General Dynamics executives, such as Dr. P.W. Lett, a Vice President of General Dynamics Land Systems, but also included non-US members in the person of General Israel Tal, the originator of the Israeli Merkava tank and Sven Berge, the designer of the Swedish S-tank, as well as myself. Both were old friends of mine which made it all the more satisfying to take part in the discussions with them that ranged widely, from the problems of NBC (Nuclear, Biological, Chemical) protection of tank crews to the fuel requirements of armoured divisions and included such contemporary topics as electric transmissions and liquid propellant guns. Meetings of TAG took place regularly until 1993 and I flew once or twice each year to Detroit to attend them.

The three non-US members of General Dynamics' Technical Advisory Group pose at a TAG meeting in Detroit in August 1993:
(left to right) Sven Berge, General Israel Tal, and RMO.

My last visit to the United States took place at the beginning of 2001, six months before the 9/11 terrorist attacks on New York and the Pentagon. The visit was a consequence of a transformation of the US Army, first proposed in 1999 by its Chief of Staff, General E. Shinseki, into a force that would be more mobile strategically. The transformation called for relatively light, air-transportable armoured vehicles and, as no existing vehicles met fully its requirements, the US Army decided to adapt a vehicle already in use to serve as its IAV, pending the production of vehicles designed specifically for it.

A variety of existing vehicles was considered but eventually the choice was whittled down to two. One of them was an eight-wheeled armoured carrier originally designed in Switzerland by the Mowag company as the Piranha III, an earlier generation of which had already been produced under license in Canada by General Dynamics for the US Marine Corps. The other was a tracked armoured carrier which was being developed from the M113 by United Defense (UD), a spin-off from FMC Corporation.

Not surprisingly, the US Army opted for a vehicle which was rated as fully developed, and therefore chose General Dynamics' wheeled carrier solution as its IAV. Moreover, it was widely - and wrongly - believed at the time that wheeled armoured vehicles were more mobile, overall, than tracked vehicles. The preference for wheeled vehicles was reinforced by the 1999 Kosovo War, during which a Russian unit equipped with wheeled armoured carriers drove at high speed from Bosnia to seize the strategically important airport at Pristina ahead of the slower-moving NATO forces. A consequence of it was that the "operational march to Pristina" became a US Army measure of the effectiveness of light armoured vehicles.

Nevertheless, UD challenged the selection of the General Dynamics' IAV. Its protest went before the US General Accounting Office (GAO) and I was retained by it as an expert witness, which involved travelling twice to Washington to appear at the GAO hearings and speaking in favour of UD's tracked vehicles. In the event, UD's protest was rejected but I considered that some of the arguments deployed in favour of General Dynamics' IAV were unconvincing and biased.

Having received an order for it, General Dynamics began to produce the IAV in 2002, when it was named Stryker. It was subsequently deployed in counter-insurgency operations in Iraq and then in Afghanistan, where it proved vulnerable to IEDs (Improvised Explosive Devices - mainly improvised blast mines) and to other threats, and its mobility was largely confined to roads.

The US Army chose the LAV III, a General Dynamics-produced version of Mowag's Piranha III, to fulfill its Interim Armored Vehicle requirement in 2000. It was subsequently named Stryker, shown here in its M1126 infantry carrier variant armed with a Kongsberg M151 remote weapon station.

Development of purpose-built vehicles to succeed the IAVs under the overarching Future Combat Systems (FCS) programme was launched in 2003. At first it was envisaged that these would be wheeled but it was soon realised that tracked vehicles represented a far more appropriate solution: indeed, all the FCS vehicles that were actually designed were tracked.

However, the whole FCS programme was terminated in 2009 without any of its constituent vehicles completing their development, as it became obvious - as it should have been before it even started - that the weight of the armour protection they needed was incompatible with the carrying capacity of the available transport aircraft, which were mainly Lockheed C-130s.

Chapter 5
Observing tank development in Israel and advising in Turkey

My connection with the Middle East began with an introduction by Sir Basil Liddell Hart, who had recently visited Israel, to the Commander of the Israeli Armoured Corps, Brigadier Elazar, when he was visiting London in 1964. He invited me to visit Israel as the guest of his Corps and of the Ordnance Corps. At the time that I received the invitation, the State of Israel and its armed forces had been created only 16 years earlier, when the Israeli kibbutz - or collective farms - repelled an onslaught by Arab armies.

The visit began in Tel Aviv. There I stayed at the Dan Hotel right on the shores of Mediterranean and gave a lecture on armoured vehicles at the headquarters of the Israeli Ordnance Corps. I was taken on a tour of Haifa and Acre which was followed by a visit to Metula, the northernmost Israeli settlement at the foot of the Golan Heights. The latter were then in Syrian hands, with the Syrian Army trenches overlooking Metula clearly visible on their slopes. The tour continued to Nazareth and to Megiddo, where according to the Bible the final battle would take place between the forces of good and evil.

After a break I was driven South through the Negev Desert to Eilat, a port and resort at the head of the Gulf of Aqaba which constitutes Israel's only access to the Red Sea. On the way back I was able to visit the very interesting ruins of Avdat, a Nabatean city which flourished in the desert until the 7th century when it was destroyed by an earthquake. One of its features, which must have made life in the middle of the desert easier, was that its cave dwellings were carved out of the rock on which it stood to face the direction of the prevailing wind. In consequence they caught the slightest breeze which made the interior of the caves feel as if they were air-conditioned even when it was hot outside. On my return to Tel Aviv I was taken to Jerusalem, but because it was divided at the time I could only view the Old City from a distance, through a barbed wire fence and at the risk, as happened to some tourists, of being shot at by the Jordanians who were occupying the City.

Brigadier David Elazar, who was RMO's pilot on a hair-raising flight over the Sinai desert. (IDF Spokesperson)

An Israeli Centurion during the 1973 Yom Kippur War (IDF)

Major General Israel Tal ('Talik') in his pomp as an armoured division commander, standing in front of an Egyptian T-55 tank captured during the 1967 Six-Day War. (IDF)

One of the British Army Chieftains loaned for a trial by the IDF in 1967 is inspected by Major General Tal. This version does not have the enlarged fuel tanks at its rear that were incorporated in the improved Chieftain Mk4 demonstrators later constructed in response to specific Israeli requirements. (Tank Museum)

In between visiting the various sights I flew with Brigadier Elazar to Beersheba to attend a firing demonstration by some recently acquired British-built Centurion tanks, which brought up to date the equipment, in part at least, of the Israeli Armoured Corps, and was then shown a rapid-reaction mobilisation depot of a tank unit with all its vehicles fully stowed with ammunition, filled with fuel and provided with all the necessary equipment, including crews' uniforms, so that they could be brought into action at very short notice by reservists recalled to man them - the Israel Defense Forces (IDF) having to rely on reservists to a considerable extent as Israel could not afford a large standing army. The atmosphere in which all this took place is illustrated by my low-level flight with Brigadier Elazar in a Piper light aircraft during which we scanned the sky for any marauding Egyptian fighter plane, although fortunately none appeared.

During the latter part of my visit I delivered lectures in Tel Aviv to senior officers of the Armoured Corps and to the Ordnance Corps. I also had a meeting with General Yitzhak Rabin, the Chief of Staff of the IDF who, among others, mentioned that he must be the only head of an army to receive daily reports on the state of the water supply, mainly from the Jordan river, which was essential to the wellbeing of Israel. The importance of the water supply was emphasized shortly after my visit, when the Syrians actually tried to divert water from the Jordan. This could have had very serious consequence for Israel and to avoid them the Syrian earth moving tractors had to be driven away from the river. Bombing them from the air might have led to a major international incident and so Brigadier (later General) Tal, who succeeded Brigadier Elazar as Commander of the Armoured Corps and whom I met during my visit in Israel in 1964 and subsequently in London, instead proposed the use of very long-range tank fire to drive off the Syrian tractors. He himself acted as the gunner in one of the two tanks which were used to fire at progressively longer range, well beyond that of the usual tank fire. The fire gradually drove the Syrian tractors away from the river and put an end to the attempts to divert the water of the Jordan.

The last lecture which I delivered during my 18-day visit was in Tel Aviv and was attended by senior IDF officers including General Rabin and also by Shimon Perez, the Deputy Minister of Defence, both of whom were to become Prime Ministers of Israel. Much of my lecture related to the recently revealed British Chieftain tank which represented a major advance in contemporary tank design and therefore aroused considerable interest. I do not know what other impact my lecture might have had on my audience but, unknown to me at the time, negotiations began two years later between Israel and Britain about further, joint development of the Chieftain. Two tanks were consequently sent from Britain to Israel for trials but in 1969, under pressure from Arab countries, the British government reneged on the agreement with Israel and the programme to jointly develop the Chieftain came to an end.

The fiasco of the British-Israeli tank cooperation and the inability to buy new tanks anywhere led to a decision by the Israeli government in 1970 to produce an indigenous tank. This came to be called Merkava, or Chariot, and the direction of its development was entrusted to General Israel Tal. Under his direction development of the Merkava made rapid progress, despite being the first tank ever to be designed and built in Israel and despite the disruption caused by the 1973 Yom Kippur War. It combined an uprated version of the engine and transmission of the US M60 tank and a US/British 105mm rifled tank gun with a unique, thickly armoured, front-engined chassis which made it one of the most effective tanks of its period.

The first Merkava was delivered to the IDF in 1979. Others followed and they received their baptism of fire in 1982, when the Israeli forces invaded southern Lebanon to bring to an end the terrorist activities of the Palestine Liberation Organisation (PLO) operating from it. This led to the invasion being called "Peace for Galilee".

As well as providing a successful baptism of fire for the Merkava, the 1982 invasion of the Lebanon was also the very first occasion on which explosive reactive armour, or ERA, was used on any tank. This type of armour, which can greatly reduce the penetration of armour by the jets of the shaped charges within rocket or missile warheads

An M60A1 tank upgraded in Israeli service with Rafael's Blazer ERA suite, based on the concept for protection against shaped-charge attack devised by Professor Manfred Held of Germany. Analoguous add-on armour was subsequently developed in Russia for Soviet tanks. (Bukvoed)

and thereby increase the protection of tanks, was devised in the mid-1960s by Professor Manfred Held. I lectured with him several years later, when he described to me how he had arrived at the idea of ERA while employed by Messerschmitt-Boelkow-Blohm (MBB), the German aerospace company involved in the development of anti-tank guided missiles. At MBB's behest he went to Israel to study the effect of shaped charges on the Soviet-built Arab tanks captured by the IDF during the Six Day

War of 1967. His ideas were taken up in the 1970s in Israel itself by the Rafael Armament Development Authority which implemented them in the form of the Blazer ERA ensemble and this was fitted to Israeli Centurion and M60 tanks before they were deployed to the Lebanon. However, ERA was not fitted at the time to the Merkavas which were, apparently, considered to be so well armoured already that they did not need it.

I was keen to see the Merkava as it represented a major departure from the general practice in tank design. In particular it had its engine and transmission at the front instead of the rear of the hull, which thus provided additional protection to its crew against attack from the most likely direction. At the same time Merkava had all its ammunition located at the rear of the hull where it was less vulnerable than in other tanks. A passage through the ammunition compartment combined with a door in the rear of the hull also provided an alternative and much safer exit, particularly under fire, than the usual practice of jumping down from the top of the tank, which the crews of all other tanks have to do.

Moreover, if most of the ammunition was removed, the rear of the hull could be used in an emergency to carry wounded personnel or up to six infantrymen. This led to ill-informed comments when the Merkava first appeared that it was a new kind of tank-cum-infantry carrier. In fact, it could only carry infantrymen or casualties in special circumstance - and at the cost of jettisoning most of its ammunition.

An opportunity to arrange a visit to Israel to see the Merkava arose in 1983 when I again encountered General Tal, at a symposium of the Swiss Society of Military Technology in Zurich at which we were both speaking. He agreed that I should come to Israel in the following year when the new, Mk 2 version of the Merkava would begin to be issued to the IDF. When I arrived he personally showed me how the Merkava was being built at the Tank Depot at Tel Hashomer near Tel Aviv. I was very impressed with its various features, including how quickly I could scramble from the driver's seat and out of tank through the door in the back of the hull, which I could not have done in any other tank.

Afterwards General Tal took me to visit the 7th Armoured Brigade, the IDF's best known armoured formation, on the Golan Heights which it defended heroically in 1973 during the Yom Kippur War against an onslaught by numerically superior Syrian tank forces. While on the Golan Heights I was able to drive a Merkava Mk 2 and then attended a firing demonstration at which a Merkava scored hits at far longer ranges than was generally accepted at the time, this being due in part to the emphasis which General Tal placed on tank gunnery when he was commander of the Armoured Corps.

General Tal poses with RMO before the latter's test drive aboard the enhanced Merkava Mk2 tank with its 105mm gun on the Golan Heights in 1984. Tal was a major proponent of long-range tank gunnery.

Back in Tel Aviv I visited Israel Military Industries and the Spectronix company where I became involved in discussing the possibility of developing active protection systems against anti-tank missiles, a subject not considered seriously elsewhere until several years later - except in the former Soviet Union, but developments there were not generally known in the West at the time. I was also taken, albeit briefly, to visit Jerusalem which was no longer divided.

As a result of my visit, I wrote several articles on the Merkava for British and US defence journals and gave lectures on it at the Royal Military College of Science, drawing attention to its unusual features. I also started to include in my lectures discussions of active protection systems and to write on them, my first article on the subject being published in *Jane's Defence Weekly* in 1985 – about ten years before the West's first active protection system to become operational, the Israeli Trophy, began to be developed.

By 1989 Merkava Mk 2 had been followed by the Mk 3 version and by agreement with General Tal I visited Israel again. As before, I was allowed to see Mk 3s being built at Tel Hashomer and then drove one on the Golan Heights. The Mk 3 was armed with a 120mm smoothbore gun, similar to those mounted at about the same time in the German Leopard 2 and the US M1A1 tanks (in the case of the latter this was instead of the 105mm L7-type rifled gun of the original M1), and it was provided with a more advanced form of the Merkava fire control system, which made it a very considerable advance on its predecessors in terms of effective firepower.

In 1993 I visited Israel on holiday with my wife but General Tal kindly arranged for us some very interesting sightseeing,

including a day in Jerusalem in the Old City where we visited the Church of the Holy Sepulchre and saw the Wailing Wall. We also visited Masada, the rocky plateau by the Dead Sea on which Jewish rebels against the Roman rule made their last stand in 73 AD after being driven out of Jerusalem. Looking down from the plateau it was amazing still to see the outlines of the camps built 2,000 years earlier by the Roman legion besieging Masada and the ramp by which it was stormed, when its defenders are reputed to have committed mass suicide.

We also visited the Israeli Tank Museum located at Latrun on a hill top overlooking the road from Tel Aviv to Jerusalem. The Museum was developed around a police station built before the Second World War when Palestine was a British mandate and was the scene of some bitter fighting in 1948 during the Israeli War of Independence, the scars of which have been left on it, deliberately. The Museum contained more than 160 tanks and other armoured vehicles representative of those used by the Israeli forces or captured from their enemies. They include one of the very first tanks which the Israeli Armoured Corps acquired when it was created in 1948: a Hotchkiss H.39 light tank built before the Second World War for the French Army, captured by the German Army in 1940, recovered after the War by the French Army and purchased, somehow, by the Israeli Underground in 1948!

General Tal also arranged a visit for me to the Armoured Corps School at Sayarim in the Negev, where I was able to drive a Mk 3 Merkava again, and to the Training Brigade at Shizafon. An interesting aspect of the visit to the Armoured Corps School was that most of instructors appeared to be female soldiers.

RMO receiving last-minute guidance prior to a test drive of the 120mm smoothbore-armed Merkava Mk3 at the Armoured Corps school in 1993. Note the instructor's seat installed above the turret, which also has added protection against top-attack.

Two years later I visited Israel again, to take part in the 1st International Conference on All-Electric Combat Vehicles which was held in Haifa and then to attend the

15th International Symposium on Ballistics which was being held in Jerusalem. In between these two events I revisited the Armoured Corps School, where I was given the opportunity to fire the gun of a Merkava Mk 3. The result was that I hit a target at a range of about 2,000m with each of three rounds, thanks to the excellence of Mk 3's tank gun fire control system, which reflected the progress made, particularly in Israel, in the development of fire control systems.

Until the end of the Second World War, and in most cases for some time after it, tank gunnery was based on direct, visual sighting of targets and manual elevation of guns to the estimated range of targets. But by the time Merkava Mk 3 was developed, optical and then laser rangefinders had come into use and gun elevation became controlled by analog and then digital computers which greatly increased tank gun hit probability.

An Achzarit heavy infantry assault carrier, based on a T-54/55 tank hull. (IDF)

In addition to firing from a Merkava Mk 3, I was also able during my visit to inspect a recently built Achzarit, the world's first modern, heavily armoured infantry vehicle. Achzarit was based on the chassis of captured and much modified, Soviet-built T-54 tanks and reflected General Tal's long held view that the infantry's fighting vehicles should be at least as well armoured as tanks because they are more often exposed to enemy fire at closer quarters.

No holiday complete without a visit to a tank museum: RMO and Jocelyn Ogorkiewicz at Latrun in 1999. (IDF)

In 1999 I visited Israel twice. The first visit was a holiday with my wife who much enjoyed the visit we made six years earlier. Once again General Tal very kindly arranged for us to view the ruins of Caesarea, the Roman administrative centre of Judea, and to see some Druze villages in addition to calling again at The Tank Museum at Latrun. For my part I was flown to Eilat from where I revisited the Training Brigade at Shizafon, and there I was given the opportunity to fire the latest Merkava Mk 3 BAZ. The firing was under more trying conditions than four years earlier, as it was on the move against a rapidly moving, crossing target at well over 2,000m. But, in spite of this, I hit the target with the first shot: that could only be attributed again to the excellence of Merkava's fire and gun control system which by then incorporated automatic target tracking. The latter was the first to be adopted in any Western tank, except for the Japanese Type 90 battle tank referred to later.

An MTU MT883 compact diesel on a test stand at Friedrichshafen in 1991, where this particular unit proved it could be run with a rated output of 2,250hp (1,650kW). (MTU)

On the following day I was flown to visit an armoured brigade on the Golan Heights and then, on the next day, I visited and gave a lecture at the Slavin plant of Israel Military Industries.

My second visit to Israel in 1999 followed a request by General Tal to discuss on his behalf research being pursued in Germany at the MTU company in Friedrichshafen into the protection of tank diesel engine control systems against electro-magnetic pulses and other forms of electro-magnetic interference. In consequence, I flew from London to Zurich and then took a ferry across Lake Constance to

A Merkava Mk3 BAZ, whose automatic target-tracking facility greatly eased long-range and mover-to-mover engagements. (IDF)

Friedrichshafen where I spent two days in discussions with MTU's electronics specialists. Five months later I flew to Israel to discuss with General Tal what I had learnt, having in the meantime submitted to him written reports.

MTU had by then developed what in my opinion and that of many others was, at the time, the best tank diesel engine, the 1,500 horse power, V-12, MT 883. General Tal was considering using it to power the next version of the Merkava, which would become the Mk 4. An MT 883 engine was in fact already installed for trials in a turretless Merkava chassis and I had the privilege of driving it, even ahead of some of those involved in its development, when it proved to be a major step forward in terms of acceleration and agility from the earlier versions of the Merkava.

My last visit to Israel took place in 2008. It was prompted in part by the entry into service of Merkava Mk 4, which began to be delivered to the IDF after my previous visit, and in part by the construction of the Namer heavy infantry vehicle, the first of which was completed shortly before my visit. I wanted to and was able to examine both the Mk 4 and the Namer, the latter representing a further embodiment of the concept pioneered with the Achzarit. However, it was purpose-built instead of being in part a modification of an earlier vehicle, although its design was based on a Merkava chassis, and it was even more heavily armoured than the Mk 4, as a result of which it weighed 60 tonnes.

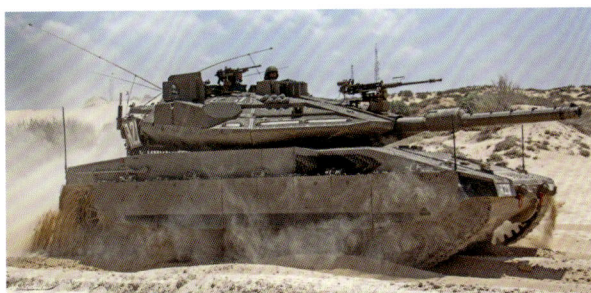

A Merkava Mk4 tank incorporating a revised powerpack based on a 1,500hp version of MTU's MT883 diesel engine. It has a shorter hull with a redesigned front engine deck and an uparmoured turret fitted with the Trophy active protection system. (IDF)

A Namer heavy infantry vehicle on trial at Fort Bliss, Texas, where the US Army conducted its own evaluation in 2012. Since 2016 the Trophy APS has been added to Namers in Israeli service. (US Army/ 1st Lt. Tyler N. Ginter)

During the visit I also called on Plasan Sasa, a company specialising in vehicle protection which was located very close to the Lebanese border, and on the Rafael Defense Systems company in Haifa. Together with my wife I also revisited Jerusalem, Caesarea, and Latrun, as well as Acre. At the end of the visit General Tal held a luncheon at which I was the principal guest and presented me with a beautifully made, scale model of the Merkava Mk 4 which became the centrepiece of my study. After the luncheon he saw me to the car which was taking me to Ben Gurion airport for the flight back to London and as we shook hands we both seemed to feel that we might not see each other again. Sadly, General Tal died two years later.

Israel Tal presents RMO with a model of his team's latest work, the Merkava 4 tank, at what proved to be their last meeting in 2008. (IDF)

Adviser in Turkey

While I was visiting Israel I was invited to advise in another Middle Eastern country, which was Turkey.

The invitation came from FNSS Savunma Sistemleri, a US-Turkish company established in 1988 in Ankara by FMC Corporation of San Jose, California, and Nurol Holdings, to produce derivatives of the M113 tracked armoured carrier, of which FMC was a large-scale manufacturer, for the Turkish Army. By 1996 FNSS also became involved in studies for the Turkish government of what would be involved in producing an indigenous tank. To pursue the studies FNSS needed help and, after some of its engineers attended a course in 1996 on armoured vehicles at the Royal Military College of Science in which I lectured, I was invited to act as an adviser to FNSS.

As an adviser I submitted a number of reports which examined candidates for the production under licence in Turkey of one of the existing tanks, as well as possible future developments, and concluded with the recommendation that the tank to be produced should be an existing and proven design. However, if the Turkish Army was not prepared to adopt an existing tank but wanted one designed

specifically for it, I then advised that its development should follow the example of the South Korean K1 which, from first hand experience, I considered particularly successful as well as being one of the most recent to be designed.

Studies of the future Turkish Army tank advanced slowly, so in 2004 and 2005 I was still writing reports on what would be required for its development. It was only in 2007 that a contract was awarded for it and it did not go to FNSS, in spite of it being the only company in Turkey with experience of producing tracked armoured vehicles. Instead the contract went to the Otokar company, which until then only produced wheeled armoured vehicles. However, Otokar secured the technical support and assistance of the South Korean Hyundai company, which produced the Korean K1 tank, as I had suggested to FNSS ten years earlier that they should do.

In the circumstances it is not very surprising that the general characteristics of the tank which Otokar designed turned out to be similar to those of Hyundai's K1A1. The first Turkish prototype was revealed in 2012 and it was called Altay, after a Turkish cavalry general of the war with Greece in the early 1920s.

The advice which I offered to FNSS was generally in the form of reports which I posted from London. But in 1997 I flew to Ankara for discussions with FNSS on their home ground and then took part on their behalf in a major, internationally supported symposium held at the Turkish Army Armor School in Ankara at which I delivered a paper on "Battle tanks in the 21st century".

I flew to Turkey again in 1999, this time to Istanbul, to speak on behalf of FNSS on armoured vehicles for the infantry at a symposium at the Turkish Army's School of Infantry at Tuzla - a part of Istanbul but on the Asiatic side of the city.

While I was in Istanbul FNSS very kindly arranged for me a tour of the principal historic sights. It started with Hagia Sophia, the massive structure built in the 6th century as a Christian church but converted after the fall of Constantinople in 1453 into a mosque and latterly a museum. The tour then took me to the elegant Blue Mosque built in the 17th century and the Topkapi palace of the sultans as well as the Grand Bazaar. I also visited the Military Museum to see a surviving section of the heavy chain stretched by the Byzantines across the Golden Horn to prevent Ottoman ships entering it, and some of the large Ottoman cannon which battered the walls of Constantinople. I also visited the Rumeli fortress built by the Ottomans at the narrowest part of the Bosphorus to stop ships sailing from the Black Sea with aid for Constantinople.

Almost as soon as I started acting as an advisor to FNSS on tanks, I was also asked to supply advice on wheeled armoured vehicles. I provided it in another series of reports, written between 1996 and 2008, on the design and performance characteristics of wheeled armoured vehicles. It transpired that FNSS was intending to expand into this particular field, which it subsequently did by adopting the Pars series of 6x6 and 8x8 vehicles designed in the United States by the General Purpose Vehicles company. Versions have since been delivered to the Turkish land forces and the Royal Army of Oman, while the DefTech AV8 Gempita, a locally produced development of the Pars 8x8, is in production for the Malaysian Army.

○
Indonesia's Kaplan medium tank, a collaboration between Turkey's FNSS and local company Pindad. (Pindad)

I was also asked to report on guns and cannon available for arming or rearming light or medium-weight armoured vehicles, such as the obsolescent French-built AMX 13 light tanks used by the Indonesian forces and the Kaplan medium tank, developed by FNSS in collaboration with the Indonesian Pindad company. This incorporated a turret with a 105mm gun made in Belgium by CMI Defence.

In addition to Israel and Turkey I also visited, although very briefly, another country in the Middle East, which was Jordan. The object of my visit there, in 2003, was to see an unconventional experimental tank turret designed and built by the King Abdullah Design and Development Bureau (KADDB) located in Amman.

The turret, which was called Falcon II, represented a revival of the concept of a low frontal-area turret which would present a smaller target to enemy fire than conventional tank turrets. The concept had last attracted interest in the 1980s, at least one attempt having been made at the time in the United States to implement it. This took the form of the so-called Tank Test Bed which General Dynamics Land Systems based upon the chassis of the M1 tank which it was then producing, but the attempt proved unsuccessful. In the case of the Falcon II turret, this was mounted on the chassis of one of the second-hand Challenger 1 tanks acquired by Jordan from Britain but its development did not proceed beyond trials. My stay in Jordan was short but in spite of this I managed to visit the interesting ruins of a Roman theatre in Amman and of a citadel on a hill overlooking it.

○
The General Dynamics Land Systems Tank Test Bed based on an M1 Abrams chassis was part of a renewed investigation in the 1980s of the low frontal-area turret, fitted with a 120mm smoothbore gun. Its appearance followed that of the US Army's short-lived M60A2 tank variant which had also featured a low frontal-area turret, embodying a 152mm hybrid gun/missile launcher. (GDLS)

○
A Challenger 1 chassis fitted with the Falcon II low-profile turret developed by Jordan's KADDB in association with South Africa's Mechanology Design Bureau in 2003. It incorporated a Swiss RUAG 120mm CTG L50 smoothbore gun and Curtiss Wright all-electric gun and turret drives, plus an autoloader developed by the FHL Division of Claverham in the UK. (KADDB)

Chapter 6
Lecturing on tanks in China, Japan and Singapore and taking part in their development in South Korea

My contacts with China began with an introduction in 1977 or 1978 by the Swiss defence attaché in London to his Chinese counterpart. The latter was probably a general but was referred to as "Mr" because the People's Liberation Army, or PLA, of which he was an officer, had not fully recovered at the time from the inanities of Mao's Cultural Revolution and restored the use of military ranks and titles.

I made further contacts in 1979 when a PLA and Chinese defence-industry delegation visited the Marconi Command and Control Systems company. I, as a consultant to Marconi, accompanied the delegation in Leicester and at the Royal Armoured Corps Gunnery School at Lulworth in Dorset, as well as giving lectures in London, as mentioned in Chapter 2.

Some months later I received an invitation to visit China. I flew there with the Chinese flag-carrier CAAC which did not at the time operate to Britain, so that I had to go first to Frankfurt where I boarded one of CAAC's Soviet-built Ilyushin Il-62 jet airliners which flew via Bucharest in Romania, where the airport seemed to be full of armed guards. From there, to avoid entering Soviet airspace which was closed to international flights, it flew over the Black Sea, northern Iran and Afghanistan to Urumchi in Western China, where it landed to refuel, and then over the Gobi Desert, to Beijing.

In China I was the guest of the Beijing Institute of Technology, the country's premier, defence-oriented academic institution. There I gave a series of six lectures on different aspects of the design and development of tanks and other armoured fighting vehicles. The lectures were held on separate days and each was attended by about 200 academics from the Institute; engineers from the North Industries Corporation, or NORINCO, which has been China's leading producer of tanks; and officers of the PLA.

As not many members of the audience could be expected to speak English and I certainly did not speak Mandarin, I was asked to send copies of the text of my lectures in advance of my visit so that it could be translated and distributed before the lectures. Each lecture took half a day and with the generous use of 35mm slide illustrations they went well. So much so that after I delivered the lectures in

Beijing I was asked if I could stay longer in China than originally arranged and repeat the lectures in Shanghai. Very much to my regret I could not do this because I had to return to London for the beginning of the academic year at Imperial College, where I was a lecturer.

However, after my visit, Beijing Institute of Technology printed my lectures and distributed them in the form of a monograph. I also conducted a number of seminars at the Institute and visited the Academy of Armor Technology. There I gave a lecture to an audience again of about 200, this time consisting of officers of the PLA, and led discussions as well as inspecting, on a separate occasion, a tank and a tracked armoured personnel carrier which represented the contemporary equipment of the PLA.

PLA Type 59 tank (top) and Type 63 APC (bottom) presented for inspection at the Chinese Academy of Armor Technology in 1979. (RMO)

The tank I saw was a Type 59 which was a clone of the Soviet T-54, a tank of 36 tonnes armed with a 100mm gun. It was the first tank to be produced in China, following the establishment in the 1950s, with Soviet assistance, of its tank manufacturing industry. When I saw it in 1979, the Type 59 was no longer in the forefront of tank development, little progress having been made during the Cultural Revolution which lasted from 1966 to 1976. This happened in spite of the PLA capturing, during the 1969 Sino-Soviet border conflict, a more advanced Soviet T-62 tank armed with a more-powerful 115mm smoothbore gun, which began to replace the T-54 in Soviet service in 1961. Thus, production of the Type 59 continued until 1980 and it remained in service into the 2000s, with the PLA as well as a number of Asian and African countries to which it was exported.

The armoured carrier I was shown was a Type 63, or YW 531. It was the first tracked armoured vehicle designed and built in China without foreign help and was somewhat rudimentary, but it represented an important first step in the development of this type of armoured vehicle. Since my visit, the PLA has in fact caught up with developments elsewhere and acquired up-to-date tanks and armoured infantry fighting vehicles, inspired to a large extent by Russian designs.

In between the lectures, seminars and discussions, Beijing Institute of Technology very generously arranged for me to be taken to see of the principal sights in Beijing. The first to be visited was the most impressive Imperial Palace or Forbidden City; then on another day I was shown around the Great Hall of the People where major political events take place, and I was also taken to Mao's Mausoleum located nearby in Tiananmen Square. On yet another day I was taken to see the Summer Palace, which still bore marks of the vandalism of the Western troops who occupied it in 1900 after crushing the Boxer Rebellion, and to the 12th century Marco Polo bridge on which Chinese and Japanese troops clashed in 1937, starting the Sino-Japanese War that went on until 1945.

I was also taken to see the very attractive Temple of Heaven and the magnificent Ming tombs. On another occasion I was driven to Badaling, which is some distance north of Beijing and to which visiting foreign dignitaries are usually taken, for a short walk along the Great Wall.

I was disappointed with the Beijing Military Museum which did not do justice to Chinese military history. Almost all that was of interest in it was a display of Vietnamese equipment captured during the brief border war with Vietnam at the beginning of 1979, some of which may have been supplied originally to Vietnam by China.

I stayed in Beijing at the Min Zu hotel, which appeared to be one of the only two Western-style hotels in the city at the time and which, it was said, was originally built to accommodate Soviet advisers who came to help the development of China's defence industry in the 1950s. As an official visitor I had a car - a Chinese-built Mercedes saloon - and driver assigned to me but there were, in general, very few cars on the streets. On the other hand there were shoals of cyclists. Some street corners were guarded by soldiers with bayonets on their rifles but there was no obvious reason for them as the crowds were peaceful and orderly.

The whole visit passed in a very friendly atmosphere and at the end of it my hosts generously presented me with two very attractive specimens of traditional Chinese art. One of them was a large, 84cm x 50cm, feather painting of a tiger, while the other was a pair of very attractively decorated vases. I greatly appreciated the gifts but, having observed how luggage is handled at airports, I became concerned about the painting, which was glass-fronted, arriving undamaged in London. However, I should not have worried as CAAC arranged the painting's safe delivery to my house, where it has been hanging in my study ever since.

Like the inward flight, my outward flight was with CAAC. It still avoided Soviet airspace but followed a very different, more direct path, from Beijing over the Himalayas to Karachi in Pakistan and then on to Paris. I did not visit China again, but for more than ten years after my visit I retained social contacts with the Chinese Embassy in London and corresponded with the Beijing Institute of Technology.

RMO closely escorted by a band of egalitarian disciples from the People's Liberation Army, some evidently more equal than others. His oratory may have left them unmoved as neither party spoke the others language.

Adviser in South Korea

A year before I flew to China I became involved in the development of tanks in another Far Eastern county, namely South Korea. This arose out of a decision by South Korea's President Park before he was assassinated in 1979 that, faced with the threat of aggression by North Korea, his country needed more powerful, indigenous tanks than those supplied hitherto by the United States. However, at the time South Korea lacked the knowledge and experience to produce one on its own and it therefore turned to companies in other countries for help. This led in the first instance to discussions with the German Krauss-Maffei company which proposed two alternative, 30- and 45-tonne, designs, based on the Leopard 1 tank that it produced at the time. However, neither alternative was accepted.

The US Defense Advanced Research Projects Agency (DARPA) then stepped in and, in collaboration with the Joint US Military Assistance Group - Korea (JUSMAG-K), brought in four US companies which, in spite of some of their names, were all involved in one way or another with tanks: Aircraft Armaments Inc. (AAI), National Water Lift (NWL), Teledyne Continental Motors (TCM) and Chrysler Defense. At the same time DARPA contracted BDM Corporation to independently evaluate the competing companies' designs. I had already worked with BDM on some US programmes and was glad to accept an invitation to join the evaluation team - on which, incidentally, I became the only non-US citizen.

The designs produced by the four companies led to a review meeting in Korea at the beginning of 1978, to which I travelled on a British Airways flight. This, like the Chinese flights described earlier, had to avoid Soviet airspace - but in its case followed the North Polar route with a stop at Anchorage in Alaska before proceeding to Tokyo from where I continued to Seoul. As the plane landed at Seoul's Kimpo Airport, I noticed that at the sides of the runways were 40mm Bofors anti-aircraft guns which were an indication of the tension at the time between South and North Korea.

In Seoul I met General Oh of the Republic of Korea Army, who was in charge of the tank project and Mr Chung, the managing director of the Hyundai company which was to produce whichever design was chosen. Both attended the presentations by the four companies as well as taking part in the discussions, as did others including members of the Agency for Defence Development, or ADD, the South Korean equivalent of the US DARPA. The outcome of it all was a decision to eliminate from the project two of the four companies. One of them was National Water Lift because its unconventional design, involving an external pedestal-mounted gun, was

considered too problematic. The other company was Chrysler Defense, which offered nothing better than a slightly modified version of the existing US M60 tank it was then producing.

The remaining two designs, by AAI and TCM, were recommended for further development and were the subject of a follow-on meeting in Seoul later in 1978. I flew to it with Korean Airlines (from Brussels instead of Paris, because of fog), which like the previous British Airways flight, landed at Anchorage en route to Seoul. The meeting was attended this time by representatives of the Hughes Aircraft Company which was offering its advanced fire control system and the French SFIM company which, similarly, was offering its stabilised periscopic sights. The meeting also included a visit to the Blue House, Seoul's equivalent of Washington's White House, to inform the officials there of what was happening.

Another meeting took place in Seoul in 1979, to which I flew with TWA to New York and then continued with Korean Airlines, stopping again en route at Anchorage. Extensive discussions were held at JUSMAG-K with General Oh and I flew with the evaluation team to Pusan for a visit to the Hyundai plant at Changwon where the proposed tank was to be built. However, although the meeting lasted more than a week, no decision was taken by the end of it to adopt either the AAI or the TCM proposal as the basis of what came to be called the Republic of Korea Indigenous Tank, or ROKIT. There was dissatisfaction with the AAI proposal because of the number of design deficiencies found within it and also with the TCM proposal because the latter was produced by a small design team considered to be insufficient to support a major tank project.

The Korean authorities then decided to abandon the approach they had pursued until then and to proceed on their own, which led them to issue an invitation directly to Chrysler Defense to produce a new proposal. At the same time they retained only myself and a retired senior tank designer from the US Army Tank-Automotive Command to evaluate the proposal. Chrysler Defense responded to the invitation in 1980 with a proposal which was very different from that it had produced two years earlier. In fact it drew on the latest experience gained in designing for the US Army what was to become the M1 Abrams battle tank and designed for South Korea one which was as good, or even better in some respects, than the latter.

But, good as it was, the design of ROKIT which Chrysler Defence produced to Korean requirements was open to improvement; I took advantage of the rapport I established with General Oh and the Hyundai management to suggest a number of them. One was to reshape the front of the hull, which originally was a copy of that of the US M1 tank, in order to gain more foot-room and better vision for the driver. I also strongly recommended making the turret larger than originally specified because ROKIT was bound to be re-armed, as indeed it was, at some stage with a larger-calibre 120mm gun in place of the 105mm gun originally specified, as had been the case with the initial version of the US M1 tank. Following British tank design practice, I also advocated not carrying any ammunition in the turret above the turret ring, in order to reduce the chances of it being hit and exploding. I also repeatedly tried to recommend the adoption of electric gun controls as being safer than hydraulic controls, but the latter were retained in line with the prevailing US design practice.

The most significant contribution I was able to make to the design of ROKIT was to persuade everybody that it should be powered by a new, German, MTU MB 871 V-8 diesel instead of the originally specified air-cooled Teledyne AVDS 1790 V-12 diesel, with which the Koreans were very familiar because of the use of similar engines in their US-built tanks. The MB 871 was superior in several respects and I established that it could be exported from Germany because it was no longer going to be used by the Bundeswehr as a result of the collapse of the Anglo-German-Italian SP70 155mm self-propelled gun project for which it was originally developed. So, on my advice, it was eventually adopted.

There was no question at any time of ROKIT following the example of the US M1 tank and being powered by a gas turbine. This not only avoided the fuel inefficiency of the gas turbine but also its high production cost, which constrained the designers of the M1 in what they could spend on other components or sub-systems within the very tight budget imposed on the Abrams tank programme by US Congress. For example they could not afford to incorporate in their design the advanced fire control system developed by Hughes Aircraft or SFIM's independently stabilised sights which I backed and which were adopted for ROKIT, making it superior in this respect to the US M1.

The different features of Chrysler's ROKIT design were initially reviewed towards the end of 1980 at a meeting in Detroit to which I flew via Washington. Its conclusion was that the design was essentially sound and should be proceeded with. A second review meeting was convened at the beginning of 1981 and I flew to Detroit again to attend it. It included the viewing of a full-size wooden mock up of ROKIT and confirmed the recommendation made after the previous meeting. Two months later I returned to Detroit for discussions with Chrysler Defence and then proceeded, via Honolulu, to Seoul. There, after meetings with General Oh and others, I wrote with my colleague our final report which we submitted to the South Korean Ministry of National Defense (MND). It concluded that the design proposed by Chrysler Defence should be accepted and recommended that an early decision be taken to put it into production in order not to lose the lead which it offered.

The 105mm-gun armed K1 tank developed for the Republic of Korea Army under the ROKIT programme, based on a General Dynamics/Chrysler design. Its propulsion and fire control was superior to its US progenitor's. (US Army/Sgt Christopher Kaufmann)

The prototype of what was no longer called ROKIT but was designated the K1 tank was, in fact, built in 1982. Production began two years later, putting to shame the time taken to reach the same stage by other tank programmes. In 1986 the K1 was developed further into the K1A1 which, as I anticipated, was rearmed with a more-powerful 120mm smoothbore gun. This, combined with the features already incorporated in the original K1 version, made K1A1 one of the Western world's most advanced tanks.

The up-gunned K1A1 model incorporates a Korean copy of the Rheinmetall 120mm L44 smoothbore gun. For hunter-killer engagements both the K1 and K1A1 incorporate a Sagem/SFIM VS580 independently stabilized panoramic sight, visible at the commander's station installed immediately behind the gunner's primary sight. (Hyundai)

My involvement in the Korean tank programme came to an end with the acceptance of the Chrysler Defense proposal but, as it did, General Oh presented me with an attractive replica of the crown of a medieval Korean king in recognition of my contribution to it.

I did not visit Korea again for ten years, when I went to support a Royal Ordnance team conducting a seminar and discussions of its products in Seoul with representatives of the Korean defence industry, prior to supporting similar Royal Ordnance activities in Japan. I also took advantage of travelling to Japan and Korea with Royal Ordnance to stay on my own in Tokyo for several days, during which I visited the Fuji School (the Japanese armoured force school) and a number of historic sights. Then, after the short stay in Seoul, I took a British Airways flight back to London, which this time involved a stop in Hong Kong and took a total of 19 hours.

I visited South Korea once more a year later, this time in response to an invitation from its Agency for Defense Development to deliver a series of lectures on tanks. This time I combined the visit to Korea with one to Australia, which I mention in Chapter 7, to where I flew to start with and whence I subsequently flew across the Pacific to Tokyo and then to Seoul. From there I travelled to the headquarters of the ADD at Taejon, about 150 km from Seoul, where I

delivered a series of lectures and conducted seminars on different aspects of the design and development of tanks. In the course of the discussions that followed I was pleased to find that the ADD engineers had already acquired a copy of my book on the "Technology of Tanks", which was published only a few months earlier, and were studying it.

RMO in full flow, lecturing a South Korean audience at the Agency for Defense Development, Taejon, in 1992.

After delivering the lectures I spent two days sightseeing. This included, among others, visiting the shrine of one of Korea's heroes, Admiral Yi Sun-chin who in the 16th century defeated an invading Japanese fleet using "turtle ships" which were peculiar to Korea and which were probably the world's first iron clad warships. I then returned to Seoul from where I flew back directly to London with Korean Airlines, which was now able to fly over Russia because the Cold War had come to an end.

Visiting Japan

In terms of correspondence with individuals, my contacts with the development of tanks in Japan go back to the 1950s. In fact, the information volunteered by one of them at the time enabled me to include a comprehensive account of the development of Japanese tanks prior to and during the Second World War in my first book on tanks. However it was not until 1978 that I visited Japan for the first time and learnt about Japanese tank development at first hand.

The first visit came about as a result of my involvement in the South Korean tank development programme described earlier in this chapter. This included a flight to Seoul with a stop in Tokyo and I took advantage of it to extend it for a couple of days, during which I called on the British Embassy for a meeting with Japanese officials and visited the controversial Yasukuni shrine dedicated to all who died in Japan's wars. A week later, on the way back from South Korea, I stopped again in Tokyo for a slightly longer stay.

Its principal feature was a visit to the factory of Mitsubishi Heavy Industries at Sagamihara, where the Type 74 tank was being produced for the Japanese Ground Self Defense Force, or JGSDF - a somewhat long winded designation which appears to have been adopted by the Japanese Army to mollify the pacifists and its political enemies.

○
Iwao Hayashi, chief design engineer of Mitsubishi Heavy Industries' tank division, responsible for Type 74 and Type 90 tank development.

The visit to Sagamihara was arranged by Iwao Hayashi who was the chief design engineer of the Mitsubishi tank division and who I met when he visited Britain and corresponded with for a number of years. He was involved in the development of the Type 74 and arranged for me to examine one and to be driven in it, as well as having lunch with a Vice President of Mitsubishi and delivering a two-hour lecture during the visit.

○
Japan's compact second-generation Type 74 tank, accepted for production in 1974, was advanced for its day, with a hydropneumatic variable suspension system, computerized fire control with laser rangefinder, and a 750hp two-stroke air-cooled diesel engine. Main armament was the British L7A3 105mm rifled gun.

The Type 74 was the second tank to be produced in Japan since the Second World War and unlike its predecessor, the first-generation Type 61, it compared favourably with European tanks, such as the German Leopard 1 and French AMX 30, which preceded it by a few years. In fairness

to the Type 61, this was designed when Japan's defence industry was still recovering from its dissolution brought about by the short-sighted policy adopted by the United States after the surrender of Japan in 1945. It was only after the outbreak of the Korean War of 1950-53 and the awakening to the threat of Soviet aggression that the earlier US policy was abandoned and Japan could begin to rebuild its defence industry and rearm itself.

While I was in Tokyo I was taken to see the gigantic, 13m high, 13th century bronze statue of Kamakura Buddha, and took a short journey in what was at the time a novelty - a 200km/h "Bullet Train".

In 1981 I visited Japan again, on the way back from meetings in Detroit and Seoul. During my stay in Tokyo I gave another lecture at the British Embassy to invited Japanese defence officials and paid a visit to the National Defense Academy at Yokosuka. There I also visited the British-built battleship *Mikasa* which took part in the 1905 battle of Tsushima when a Russian fleet was destroyed, and is now in drydock as a memorial ship. I also had the great pleasure of meeting Lieutenant General Tomio Hara, who as a young engineer officer in the Imperial Japanese Army designed the first Japanese tank, having nothing to go on except for some First World War British Medium A and French Renault FT tanks which the Japanese Army had purchased for trials. Nevertheless, the tank he designed was successfully built in 1927 and was the foundation of Japanese tank development in which he was involved almost until the end of the Second World War. He was at that time, he told me, reduced to serving as an inspector in an aircraft factory instead of being involved in tank production, because of a shortage of steel for tanks. I had corresponded with General Hara for a number of years and helped the publication in Britain of his accounts of the development of Japanese tanks up to the end of the Second World War in a series of booklets entitled *AFV Profiles*. He, in turn, presented me with a number of books he had published in Japan on tanks, which I subsequently deposited in the archives of The Tank Museum at Bovington.

It was only ten years later that I paid another visit to Japan. This time it was by a direct flight from London to Tokyo, over Russia, instead of the North Polar route with a stop at Anchorage. On arrival in Tokyo I was met by Iwao Hayashi who personally took me to sightsee in Kyoto, to see the Golden and other temples, and then to Osaka where we visited its formidable castle before going on to Kobe and returning to Tokyo. There I joined the Royal Ordnance team which was visiting the Sumitomo corporation to acquaint it with its products and took part in seminars at the British Embassy attended by officers of JGSDF and representatives of the Japanese defence industry.

Following the meetings I visited the Fuji School, the training centre for Japanese armoured forces, located at the foot of Mount Fuji, Japan's highest mountain. I was very cordially greeted by the general commanding the School and was shown as well as being driven in a Type 90 tank, which had just been unveiled after being adopted by the JGSDF. In addition I was shown the new Type 89 infantry fighting vehicle. For my part I delivered a lecture on tanks.

RMO taking a ride in Japan's third-generation Type 90 tank at the JGSDF armour training centre, Mt Fuji, in November 1991.

Type 90 proved to be not only abreast of the latest tanks built elsewhere but even ahead, in some respects, of the most advanced of them. It was for example ahead of all other tanks, including the Israeli Merkava, in incorporating automatic target tracking in its fire control system, which I was given an opportunity to operate. However, in spite of all its advanced features, Type 90 proved to be something of a disappointment for the JGSDF because it weighed 50 tonnes, which made it too heavy for much of the Japanese transportation system and therefore constrained its operational and strategic mobility. In consequence, it was followed by the development of the Type 10 tank which was very similar but had part of its armour removable so that its weight could be reduced to 44 tonnes.

The Type 90 (left) seen alongside its smaller counterpart, the Type 10 tank, which is better adapted to Japanese bridge classifications. (Los668)

From Tokyo I flew with the Royal Ordnance team to Seoul and then back to London, via Hong Kong, as I already mentioned.

Lecturing in Singapore

The last of my visits to the Far East was to Singapore. I went there after coming into contact in the mid-1980s with the then Singapore Technology Corporation, which became responsible for the development of armoured vehicles in Singapore. This led to correspondence and to discussions with some of its engineers when they visited Britain. Most of these contacts related to tanks, which the Singapore Army had acquired following the formation of its first armoured regiment in 1968, only three years after Singapore gained its independence. The regiment was formed with the covert assistance of Israeli military personnel and was equipped with 60 second-hand AMX 13 light tanks purchased from Israel. Singapore also acquired 200 AMX 13 from Switzerland and some more from Austria; this brought the total to 470 and they formed the largest fleet of AMX 13 tanks that were still operational of the 2,800 originally built in France.

To modernise them and to improve their capabilities, Singapore Technology retrofitted the AMX 13 tanks with diesel engines, automatic transmissions and hydropneumatic suspensions and developed more effective armour-piercing ammunition for their 75mm guns. The upgraded tanks, which were designated AMX 13 SMi, were still inferior to contemporary battle tanks but they met adequately the contemporary strategic requirements of Singapore and in particular its policy of deterring hostile neighbours. At the same time they introduced Singaporean forces to the use of tanks and Singaporean engineering companies to the development of armoured vehicles.

I was able to examine an AMX 13 SMi when I visited Singapore in 1990 to deliver a series of lectures on the design of tanks and other armoured vehicles. The visit lasted almost two weeks which gave me an opportunity to acquaint myself with Singapore and life within it. As a result I became impressed with what I saw of the pragmatic policies of its government and with its social system, as well as such features as its modern transportation system and clean streets, along which one could walk safely at all times - which is more than could be said of some places I visited.

The Bionix 25, the initial production version of the Singapore Technology Bionix infantry combat vehicle armed with a 25mm M242 Bushmaster cannon. (ST Automotive)

I visited Singapore again in 2000 in response to another invitation to give a series of lectures on armoured vehicle technology. During the intervening ten years I remained in contact with the Singapore Ministry of Defence (MINDEF) and with Singapore Technology, to which I was able to provide some advice and information. During this period Singapore Technology developed and began to produce a tracked armoured infantry fighting vehicle called Bionix. It was the first armoured vehicle designed and produced in Singapore, using steel armour imported from Sweden and diesel engines and transmissions procured from the United States. I was able to drive an early production Bionix when I arrived in Singapore to deliver my lectures and found it to be well up to the standard of contemporary infantry fighting vehicles, although I did not like the transmission chosen for it.

During my visit I was able to examine not only the Bionix but also a prototype of Bronco, an all-terrain articulated armoured carrier which had just been revealed. Bronco was subsequently produced for the Singaporean Army and in 2008 some were also ordered by the British Ministry of Defence for use in Afghanistan, under the name Warthog. This was somewhat ironic as it meant that the British Ministry of Defence was procuring armoured vehicles for the British Army, not from what was still left of the British armoured vehicle industry but from a recently liberated, former British colony!

Since my last visit, Singapore Technology had also produced a very capable, eight-wheeled armoured infantry carrier called Terrex, which it developed in collaboration with the Irish Timoney Technology company and which I was able to view at defence equipment exhibitions held in London. Terrex was adopted by the Singapore Army and might have been a candidate for adoption also by the British Army, particularly as it had already procured the Warthog from Singapore. But the Ministry of Defence continued to dither over the adoption of multi-wheeled armoured infantry carriers and did not order any for the British Army until 2018 [when it once again adopted Boxer], well after all other armies of any consequence had adopted them.

During my second visit to Singapore I stayed at the Stamford Westin hotel, which had only just been overtaken as the world's tallest hotel building and was indicative of the material progress that the city state was making. Before I left, my hosts also entertained me to dinner at the famous Raffles hotel, named after the founder of Singapore who established it in 1819.

The Bronco all-terrain tracked carrier in its uparmoured Warthog version supplied to the British Army. (Andrew Linnett/MoD)

Chapter 7
Participating in armoured vehicle development in Brazil, South Africa and Australia

My activities in Brazil were initiated, oddly enough, by an ex-Czech Army officer, Josef Soucek, who set up a factory in São Paulo to rework the tracks of the Brazilian Army's armoured carriers and to produce bullet-proof tyres. In the course of his activities he had come across my writings and lectures and decided to bring them to the attention of the Brazilian military authorities with which he was dealing. This prompted the latter to invite me in 1972 to visit Brazil, to lecture and to discuss the armoured vehicles they were developing.

My arrival in São Paulo aroused a surprising amount of interest in the local press which published several items on it and was followed by a very busy two-week visit. During the visit I delivered a total of four lectures on armoured vehicles, including one at the headquarters of the 2nd Army in São Paulo, another at the Arsenal da Urca on the Copacabana and two at the Instituto Militar de Engenharia (IME) in Rio de Janeiro, the second of which was attended by nine generals as well as many officers from the Staff College. In between the lectures and the discussions I was flown

for a short visit to Brasilia, the capital city newly established in the middle of the country, to see its ultra modern architecture and especially that of its cathedral. In Rio I went to the foot of the world-famous statue of Christ which overlooks the city from the top of the Corcovado mountain.

In São Paulo I met Jose Luiz Whitaker Ribeiro, the president of the Engesa Engineering Company which two years earlier took over from the Brazilian Army the development of new wheeled armoured vehicles intended to replace the M8 armoured cars built in the US during the Second World War and still used at the time in Brazil. By 1972 Engesa had already built the prototype of a six-wheeled armoured carrier which incorporated the same automotive components as a companion reconnaissance vehicle, but with the engine compartment located at the front instead of the rear of the chassis. The carrier, which was called Urutu after a poisonous Brazilian snake, was amphibious and the ability of its prototype to swim was shown to me in a demonstration at a lake near São Paulo in which I took part.

RMO aboard a prototype of Engesa's EE-11 Urutu 6x6 carrier during amphibious trials in 1972. (Engesa)

The reconnaissance vehicles, called Cascavel after another Brazilian snake, were originally fitted with manually loaded 37mm guns recovered from the M8 armoured cars, which were clearly out of date. In consequence, when Jose Ribeiro came to London a few months after my visit to Brazil I took him to the Alvis company in Coventry which produced Saladin armoured cars with turret-mounted 76 mm guns that would have made Cascavel much more effective. My suggestion that this possibility be pursued was approved by the Ministry of Defence and a Saladin turret accompanied by a British Army demonstration team was sent to Brazil in 1973. However, in the end Engesa decided to adopt the turret produced in France for the Panhard AML light armoured car which was armed with a low-pressure 90 mm gun firing fin-stabilised projectiles. Eventually, for its Cascavel III model, Engesa adopted a similar 90mm low-pressure gun developed in Belgium and produced it under licence in Brazil.

○
The Engesa EE-9 reconnaissance vehicle in its Cascavel III version, armed with the Cockerill Mk3 90mm gun, as adopted by the Iraqi Army.

There was also a case for arming the Urutu with a weapon more effective than the externally mounted machine gun with which it was fitted. I suggested that this could be done by adopting the one-man turret armed with a 20mm automatic cannon which Bofors had produced for the Swedish Pbv 302 tracked armoured carrier. Bofors agreed to send one for trials and it was mounted successfully on an Urutu but the Swedish government would not allow the sale of turrets to Brazil because of its misguided disapproval of the Brazilian military government, so nothing came of it.

The automotive components which the Cascavel and Urutu shared included a conventional, double transverse wishbone, independent suspension for the two front wheels and what Jose Juiz described as a "boomerang suspension" for the rear wheels, two of which on each side were mounted on a walking beam. The beam contained a train of gears and distributed the drive between the wheels, helping them to generate maximum traction when the vehicles operated over broken ground. A special amphibious version of the Urutu was developed for the

Fuzileiros Navais, the Marines of the Brazilian Navy, who were actually the first to place a production order for it. This version not only had a fully enclosed hull and shrouded propellers but was also provided on each side of the hull roof with a pair of air intake tubes, through which air could be drawn into the crew compartment and from it into the engine. In consequence, when the air intake tubes were swivelled into a vertical position, the roof of the hull could be washed over without the danger of the vehicle being swamped. This meant that the Marines' version of the Urutu could not only swim in calm inland waters but could also operate in rough seas with waves up to 3m high, or in heavy surf.

The hulls of the Urutu and the Cascavel as well as the turrets of the latter were all welded from special dual-hardness steel amour developed by Engesa, which was much more effective against bullets than conventional steel armour and made the two vehicles better protected in relation to their weight than other light armoured vehicles.

In 1976 I revisited Brazil, this time at the invitation of Engesa. During my visit I lectured to the Brazilian Army General Staff in Brasilia, at IME in Rio de Janeiro, and at Engesa in São Paulo. I also saw the new Engesa assembly plant near São Paulo, at São José dos Campos where full-scale production of the Cascavel and the Urutu started in 1974, and visited the machining plant which Engesa acquired in Salvador de Bahia. The latter is a city of about 300 churches, some beautifully decorated, a relic of the days when it was a prosperous centre of the slave trade and of sugarcane exports. In between, I was taken to see the Iguazu Falls, the largest waterfall system in the world on the border with Argentina, over which I was flown in a helicopter. On the following day I paid a brief visit over the border to Stroessner in Paraguay, before returning to São Paulo. At the end of the visit Engesa very generously arranged my flight back from Rio de Janeiro in an Air France Concorde supersonic aircraft, which cruised at Mach 2.0, or twice the speed of sound, on its way to Paris, landing en route at Dakar in Senegal to refuel.

Two years later I was invited to Brazil again, mainly to see Engesa's successful production of the Cascavel and Urutu. Ultimately the two armoured vehicles were procured by about 20 different countries in Latin America, Africa and the Middle East. My Engesa hosts told me that in the case of Iraq they were initially contacted about their vehicles by Iraqi army officers after they read one of my articles about them! During my visit, I lectured again at Engesa in São Paulo at the 1st Army Headquarters and IME in Rio de Janeiro, and revisited Engesa plants in São José dos Campos and in Salvador. After the visit I flew again from Rio de Janeiro to Paris via Dakar in a Concorde.

In addition to the Cascavel and Urutu, Engesa produced Jararaca, a light, turretless four- wheeled, armoured reconnaissance vehicle, and built two prototypes of Sucuri, a six-wheeled tank destroyer armed with a 105mm tank gun. The second of these advanced from the "boomerang" suspension of the earlier Engesa vehicles to an independent suspension, all round.

The successful production of the Cascavel and Urutu, which eventually came to 2,767 vehicles, led in 1982 to a decision by Engesa to develop a tank. There were to be two versions, both called Osorio after a 19th century Brazilian cavalry general. One version, which was to be offered to the Brazilian Army, was to be the simpler of the two and armed with the widely used 105mm rifled tank gun; the other version, which was intended for sale to Saudi Arabia, was to be as advanced as any contemporary tank and was to be armed with a 120mm smoothbore tank gun.

To make up in part for its lack of experience in tank development, Engesa initially hired an American tank designer - though I did not think much of his ideas when I briefly visited Brazil in 1983. I was therefore glad to learn at a meeting in London shortly after my visit with the Managing Director of Vickers Defence Systems that the latter would collaborate with Engesa. This would result in Vickers becoming responsible for the turrets and the weapon systems of the two versions, while Engesa designed and built the chassis which was to be common to both.

Engesa's Osorio T-2 tank armed with a French 120mm smoothbore gun in an adaptation of the turret of the Vickers Mk7 tank. (Engesa)

The simpler, or T-1, version of the Osorio was completed in 1985 and the other, or T-2, was completed a year later. The speed with which the two prototypes of the Osorio were designed and built was remarkable. It could be ascribed in part to Engesa being untramelled by the military bureaucracy which in some cases has prolonged the development of tanks to a ridiculous extent. Another

factor was the judicious exploitation of components or subsystems which happened to be available on the international scene. Thus the turret of the T-1 version came, in essence, from the Vickers Valiant experimental tank while that of the T-2 was originally developed for another Vickers tank, the Mk 7, which was unsuccessfully built for export but which, after being rearmed with the French (GIAT-produced) 120mm smoothbore gun instead of its original British L11 120mm rifled gun, made the T-2 version of the Osorio as well armed as any contemporary battle tank. The engine which powered both versions of the Osorio was a surprisingly successful adaptation to automotive use of a German MWM industrial diesel, while their transmission, produced in Germany by ZF, had already been adopted for the South Korean and Italian battle tanks, and their Dunlop hydropneumatic suspension was the unsuccessful contender for the suspension of the British Challenger tank.

The Vickers Mk7 export tank, fitted here with a medium-pressure L11 120mm rifled gun, was based on a Leopard 2 hull and automotive system. (Vickers)

In spite of the variety of components and their different origins, Engesa successfully integrated them all in the two prototypes and in 1985, when the T-1 was sent to Saudi Arabia for preliminary trials, it outperformed a British Challenger. In 1987 it was followed by the T-2 prototype which was sent to Saudi Arabia to take part in extensive competitive trials, in which it outperformed not only the Challenger and the French AMX 40 but proved as good as the US M1A1. On the strength of its performance, Engesa expected that the Saudi authorities would order the 316 Osorios they had indicated they would, and it continued to operate on that assumption when I visited São Paulo once more in 1987. During the visit I had an opportunity to drive the T-2 prototype which had just returned from the trials in Saudi Arabia and which I found fully up to expectations. However, the Saudi authorities failed to follow through with an order for it. Instead, in 1990, on the eve of the Iraqi invasion of Kuwait, they decided to order 315 M1A2 tanks from the United States. This undermined Engesa's financial position and deprived it of the money it required for further development of tanks and other armoured vehicles and forced it to file for bankruptcy within the year.

In consequence Engesa went into liquidation and Brazil lost the ability to produce modern battle tanks as well as other armoured vehicles. Two years later, a Brazilian accounting and consultancy firm called Trevisan set out to investigate whether Engesa could be revived and I was invited to come to São Paulo once again to take part in the consequent discussions, which became the last act in the story of Engesa. My visit also impressed upon me the deterioration of the internal security situation which had taken place in Brazil. Thus, on my first visit to Brazil 20 years earlier, when it was under a military government, one could walk safely around São Paulo. But in 1992, by which time it had reverted to civilian rule, my Brazilian friends warned me to beware of muggers, even on the principal street of São Paulo, the Avenida Paulista.

On my return to London, I submitted a report to Trevisan in which I concluded that Engesa could only be revived if the Brazilian Army ordered some Osorios. But this the Brazilian Army failed to do all along, leaving it to Engesa to finance tank development by itself.

Yet, only five years later, the Brazilian Army started to procure 128 second-hand, German-built Leopard 1A1 tanks which had been used by the Belgian Army. Some of these were in a poor condition, and consequently were of little value. It did better later when it began to acquire directly from Germany 340 second-hand Leopard 1A5s. They were well proven but in principle they were no better than the T-1 version of the Osorio and were in several respects inferior to the T-2 version. However, they could be acquired directly, without the development of the of the production facilities which the Osorio would have required.

Discussions and lectures in South Africa

To some extent my activities in Brazil overlapped with those in another country in the Southern Hemisphere, namely South Africa. They followed an introduction in France in 1973 by the Panhard company to Major General J. Dutton, who was Chief of Staff of the South African Army and its senior armour officer. This came about as a result of Panhard knowing me well on the one hand and it on the other enjoying good relations with South Africa, to which it had in the 1960s sold 100 of its AML light armoured cars and a licence to produce 500 more.

The initial contact with General Dutton was followed by an invitation from its army command to visit South Africa in 1974. I flew there with South African Airways (SAA) which was already operating Boeing 747 "Jumbo Jets"

but at the time could not fly directly from London to Johannesburg, since it could not overfly West Africa due to the hostility to South Africa of some African states. In consequence, SAA aircraft had to skirt West Africa and land on the Cape Verde islands, where they refuelled at an airport which appeared to be controlled by somewhat scruffy local militiamen who had taken it over recently from the Portuguese colonial administration.

After landing at Johannesburg, I was driven to Pretoria where on the following day I had a meeting with Lieutenant General M.A. Malan, the Chief of the South African Army. Next day I lectured on armoured vehicles at the Armament Board, which governed South African armament development and acquisition activities, and on the following day I lectured at the South African Army College. I was then flown to Bloemfontein to visit the School of Armour at Tempe where I delivered more lectures. From there I was flown by helicopter to Kimberley to see the famous "Big Hole" - an 800m deep hole dug by hand in the 19th century by diamond miners.

From Kimberley I was flown to Cape Town where, inevitably, I went to the top of the Table Mountain and from where I was driven to visit the Naval Base at Simonstown. I was then flown to Oudtshoorn to lecture at the South African Infantry School, whence I visited the Cangol Caves, world famous for their stalactites, and one of the ostrich farms which are a feature of the area and renowned for their feather exports. I then travelled on to Durban in the Natal where I met some of the South African Army stationed there and on to Empangeni to visit the Zulu University before returning to Pretoria.

From Pretoria I was flown to the Mala Mala private game reserve in the Kruger National Park where I took part in a game drive and had the opportunity to watch many different animals, ranging from elephants and hippos to lions, giraffes and zebras. I then returned to Pretoria and visited Boksburg where the Sandock Austral company was license-producing a modified version of the Panhard AML light armoured car under the name Eland

On the last day of my 19-day visit to South Africa I had a meeting in Johannesburg with General Dutton and other South African Army officers and members of the Armaments Board and then flew back to London with South African Airways. This time, for some reason, SAA landed in Luanda in Angola which was still in Portuguese hands but where the atmosphere was tense because of the impending Portuguese withdrawal and the consequent political changes. The SAA flight then proceeded to the Cape Verde islands where it landed to refuel, as before, before flying on to London.

I was invited to visit South Africa again in 1979 and flew there with SAA, which this time refuelled at Las Palmas in the Canary Islands, and then flew on to Johannesburg skirting West Africa, as before. The visit started with a meeting with the Chief of the Army which was followed by lectures at the South African Defence College, the University of South Africa and Armscor. I also made a visit to the Centre for Scientific and Industrial Research (CSIR) to see some of its pioneer work on mine-resistant vehicles. I was then flown to Bloemfontein to lecture again at the School of Armour and on to a game lodge in the Kruger National Park where I took part in another game drive. Back in Pretoria I lectured at the Defence College and at the Army College and in between re-visited Sandock Austral which was by then producing the Ratel infantry armoured fighting vehicle. I had seen a pre-production version of it briefly during my previous visit to South Africa but this time I was able to examine it in detail and to drive it.

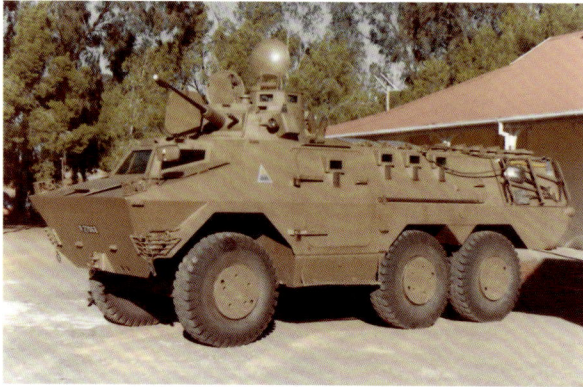

A Ratel 6x6 infantry carrier in South African Defence Force service, armed with a 20mm turret. (RMO)

Ratel was a robust, six-wheeled, truck-based armoured vehicle developed in South Africa but incorporating some automotive components surreptitiously imported from elsewhere because of the embargo on the sales of military equipment to South Africa. This was imposed at the time by the United Nations on account of its policy of racial segregation, or apartheid. Ratel proved very effective in the war which escalated in the mid-1970s on the border with Angola, against the latter's Marxist forces backed by the Soviet Union and Cuba. Eventually about 1,400 Ratels were built and some of them were later sold to a number of African countries and to Jordan.

When I was invited again in 1990, South Africa had experienced several years of a state of emergency brought about by unrest in the townships and had been more deeply involved in the Angolan War. However, this had no direct impact on my visit which this time started with a 12.5h non-stop flight from London to Johannesburg in a long-range "Jumbo Jet" which did not need to refuel en route.

On arrival, which happened to be at a week-end, I was driven to the Mabula Game Reserve and on the following day I visited the Gerotek test ground to drive a pre-production version of the Rooikat combat and reconnaissance vehicle. This advanced, eight-wheeled, 28-tonne vehicle, armed with a high-velocity 76mm gun, was the outcome of a research and development programme pursued by the South African Army since the mid-1970s, despite United Nations sanctions, and brought to fruition in 1990 when its series production began. Eventually 242 were built.

Rooikat answered the needs of the South African Army far better than a light tank would have done because of its greater operational mobility, particularly in sandy terrain. It was therefore well suited to the vast area of southern Africa over which it would have to operate. Its characteristics were also in keeping with the tradition of the harassing raids carried out by Boer commandoes during the Anglo-Boer War of 1899-1902. As a result, the type of mobile combat vehicle which Rooikat came to represent featured very prominently in the various discussions I had in South Africa about armoured vehicles.

After test-driving the Rooikat, I lectured at the Army Staff College and at the headquarters of a South African Army division located in Pretoria, before going to Boksburg to visit OMC, or the Olifant Engineering Company, which had taken over Sandock Austral and become responsible for production of the Rooikat. I then flew to Bloemfontein to give four lectures at the School of Armour and then on to Cape Town where I lectured to the 71st Brigade of the South African Army and visited the Castle, an interesting, well-preserved fort built by the Dutch in the 17th century, as well as going again to the top of the Table Mountain. From Cape Town I was flown to Kimberley and then driven 240km to Lohatla, in Northern Cape Province, to visit and to lecture at the Army Battle School located there.

2011 photograph of an Olifant 1B tank upgraded to Mk2 standard which introduced an uprated engine and a panoramic sight for the commander (not fitted here). (US Army Africom)

Back in Pretoria I conducted a seminar at CSIR and on the following day I was given an opportunity to drive a South African Olifant 1B tank. Olifant, or Elephant, was a much modified British Centurion, 200 of which were originally acquired by South Africa as part of the British Commonwealth Strategic Reserve. But when South Africa left the Commonwealth in 1961, its government saw no need for tanks and sold 100 of the Centurions to Switzerland. However, in the 1970s South Africa had to revise its view of their importance in the light of the war in Angola and, in particular, of the intervention of Cuban troops and the use by the Marxist forces of T-54 and other tanks supplied to them by the Soviet Union and its satellites. In consequence, it began to upgrade what remained of its Centurion fleet and brought it back to its original strength by rebuilding a number using salvaged hulls acquired from Jordan and India. Eventually, in the 1980s, it deployed with some success a squadron of the modernised Centurion (Olifant 1A), in the Angolan War.

Olifant was powered by a Teledyne diesel engine similar to that of the US M60 tank, which was acquired in spite of UN sanctions, and was armed with a 105mm tank gun instead of the 20pdr originally mounted in the Centurions. As in the case of the first British L7 guns, Olifant's gun tubes were produced initially by boring out the barrels of 20pdrs from 83.8 to 105mm. The engines and other automotive improvements made the Olifants very much easier to drive and their armament also made them comparable in terms of their battlefield capabilities to the Centurions upgraded in Israel two decades earlier. The latter tanks proved very effective during the Yom Kippur War of 1973, particularly in the defence of the Golan Heights against Soviet-built Syrian tanks, some of which were similar to those encountered later by the South African forces in Angola.

My next visit to South Africa in 1993 was relatively short, lasting as it for did six days. Most of them were taken with discussing the design of the Tank Technology Demonstrator (TTD), the prototype of a very modern indigenous battle tank comparable to the original version of the German Leopard 2. Its design was conceived as a safeguard against a possible future use by the Marxist forces in Angola of more modern Soviet tanks, and in particular of the T-72. Its development was a very considerable achievement in view of the fact that South Africa had not designed a tank before. Moreover, it did so in face of UN Sanctions which hampered the transfer of military technology from other countries and which were not lifted until 1994.

During my visit I saw the turret and the chassis of the TTD which was subsequently assembled. The turret was fitted with a 105mm tank gun, although provision was made in

South Africa's TTD had a turret capable of accepting either a locally produced 120mm smoothbore or 105mm rifled gun (shown here), installed on a new chassis design. (C.Foss)

its design for the installation a 120mm smoothbore gun in keeping with what was becoming general practice in Western countries. However, development of the TTD ceased to be pursued in the mid-1990s because the need for a tank of its kind disappeared with the contemporary changes in the political situation, including the collapse of the Soviet Union and the withdrawal of Cuban troops from Angola.

The prototype of the upgunned Rooikat 105 reconnaissance vehicle, which had a 105mm rifled gun in place of the 76mm rifled naval gun of the baseline Rooikat. (Denel)

In spite of the visit being relatively short, there was enough time to fly 560 miles to a range at Kakames in Northern Cape Province, not far from the border with Namibia, where I was able to drive and to fire an experimental version of the Rooikat armed with a 105mm tank gun. This gun made the experimental model much more powerful than the standard vehicles armed with a 76mm gun that was actually based on a widely sold Italian (Oto Melara) naval gun with which the South African Navy had armed some of its ships. The use of basically the same gun in armoured vehicles as well as warships greatly simplified its manufacture and logistics support and, although it was not as powerful as the 105mm tank gun, it met the requirements of the Rooikat's intended role while the more heavily armed Rooikat 105 model was not developed beyond a single experimental vehicle.

A year later I flew again to South Africa, mainly to take part in an Armour and Countermine Symposium held at the DEXSA defence exhibition. However, I also revisited the School of Armour in Bloemfontein and attended a demonstration at the Army Battle School at Lohatla.

My last visit to South Africa took place in 1996, its main object being to attend the 50th anniversary of the formation of the South African Armoured Corps. But before the celebrations of the anniversary, a South African Army friend drove me for a short stay in Sun City, a luxury resort recently built in North West Province. From there I went to Pretoria to lecture once more at the Army Staff College and then flew to Bloemfontein to speak at the Armour Symposium being held there. On the following day I was flown to the Alkantpan ballistic test range in a the semi-desert part of Northern Cape near the Namibian border, to a demonstration of the mobility of Rooikat 105 and in particular of its ability to drive at high speed without one of its front wheels, as if that had been blown off by a mine explosion.

On returning to Bloemfontein I attended the celebrations of the anniversary of the formation of the South African Armoured Corps which included a formal parade of a battalion of South African troops at the School of Armour. The salute on this occasion was taken by Nelson Mandela who had become President of South Africa following the decision by the South African government to abandon its policy of apartheid. The celebrations went on to include the opening of the South African Armour museum, which I attended representing The Tank Museum at Bovington, after which I flew back from Johannesburg to London. The flight did not have to skirt West Africa this time and consequently took only ten and a half hours.

Visiting Australia

In addition to South Africa and Brazil I was also involved, albeit briefly, with another country in the Southern Hemisphere, which was Australia.

At first this was in connection with an armoured vehicles design study which the Australian Army commissioned the British consultancy company EASAMS of Camberley to carry out between 1981 and 1983. The study was called Project Waler after a hardy Australian horse and concerned an armoured carrier which the Australian Army considered at the time developing and procuring. I was involved in it as a consultant working with design engineers from Vickers. The study covered in some detail three possible alternatives, one of which was a fairly

conventional tracked armoured carrier. Another was a wheeled carrier, while the third was an articulated tracked carrier which reflected the contemporary interest in articulated tracked armoured vehicles.

However, nothing came of it all as the Australian Army decided not to proceed with the Waler project beyond the studies. But when it was terminated I received a letter from the Australian High Commission in London thanking me for my contribution to it.

I had nothing more to do with Australia until 1992, when Australian Defence Industries (ADI) invited me to come to Canberra as a consultant, for a short visit to discuss and lecture on military vehicle technology. This I did in three days of meetings with senior Australian Army officers and members of ADI's management. On the fourth day of the visit I flew to Melbourne, from where I went to Bendigo to see ADI's manufacturing facilities and potentially the site of armoured vehicle production in Australia, which it indeed became several years later.

I took advantage of the visit to Canberra to stay in advance of it for a couple of days in Sydney with an Australian Army friend, Colonel John Lenehan, whom I first met in Britain when we were both involved in Project Waler. John's apartment overlooked Sydney Harbour and he very kindly took me to see Sydney's iconic Opera House as well as various sights around Sydney, including Bondi Beach.

At the end of the visit to Canberra, I flew via Sydney to Tokyo and then on to Seoul for a week in South Korea, where I was invited by the Agency for Defense Development (ADD) to deliver a series of presentations and seminars on armoured vehicles which are mentioned earlier in this chapter.

Epilogue

Tank-related events initially described in this book coincided with the development of tanks and other armoured vehicles that had begun towards the end of the Second World War and continued after it in three countries – the United States, Soviet Union and Great Britain – and had resumed immediately after it in France. Development then became more intense after the invasion of South Korea by North Korean forces in 1950 and the onset of the Cold War, brought about by the aggressive policies of the Soviet Union which maintained a large force of tanks.

The upsurge in the development and production of tanks in the 1950s involved not only countries already producing them but also others which had done so previously but then discontinued or were made to cease for a time their production. These countries included West Germany and Sweden and, somewhat later, Japan and Italy. What is more, tanks began to be developed in countries which had not produced them previously, such as Switzerland, and a few years later, Israel, India and South Korea. I had the good fortune to participate in the development of some of these tanks, or at least to observe it at close quarters.

Progress which the development of tanks was making suffered a short-lived setback in 1973 when, during the opening stage of the Yom Kippur War between Israel and the neighbouring Arab countries, Soviet-made anti-tank guided missiles deployed by the Egyptian infantry destroyed a number of Israeli tanks. This made some observers rush to the conclusion that the days of tanks were numbered, as had been wrongly predicted on a number of earlier occasions. In fact, tanks never had been invulnerable and tank guns proved more effective, overall, against enemy tanks in the Yom Kippur War than anti-tank guided missiles. Thus tanks came once more to be considered the best counter to other tanks.

In consequence, tank forces continued to grow in the Western countries during the 1980s as the most effective deterrent to the Soviet armoured forces poised in Central Europe. The total number of tanks which the countries of the North Atlantic Treaty Organization, or NATO, could muster remained smaller than the number of tanks possessed by the Soviet Union, which eventually amounted to 63,900 tanks, but they constituted, nevertheless, a very effective defensive force.

The situation changed dramatically with the collapse of the Soviet Union in 1989 and the subsequent withdrawal of the Soviet forces from Central Europe. This was seized by Western governments as an excuse for cutting down drastically their forces, including the number of their tanks, as part of the so-called "Peace Dividend". A striking example of the drastic cuts was provided by West Germany which cut down the number of tanks it had from 5,212 in 1989 to 225 tanks in 2011. Belgium and the Netherlands went even farther and disposed of their tanks altogether, selling them to Brazil and Chile.

Tanks were still deployed on a large scale in 1991 during the First Gulf War, fought for the liberation of Kuwait, when the US Army had 3,113 of them transported to the Middle East. But the disastrous decision of the US Government to invade Iraq in 2003 not only led to the destruction of the Iraqi army and its tank force but also changed the general situation in the Middle East, and in its aftermath attention turned away from tanks to counter-insurgency operations in Iraq and Afghanistan. The place of tanks was then taken by lighter armoured vehicles, such as armoured personnel carriers, and by semi-improvised, truck-based MRAP (Mine Resistant - Ambush Protected) vehicles which could patrol more easily along roads but which were more vulnerable and had very limited offensive capabilities. Nevertheless, the number of MRAPs which were eventually built amounted to as many as 12,000.

It was only after a breakdown a few years later of the relations with the Russian Federation - and a revival by the latter of the tank resources which it inherited from the Soviet Union - that the West began to pay more attention, once again, to tanks. But this did not lead to any significant attempts to rebuild their numbers. In fact, the British Army planned to reduce further the number of the tanks that it kept, to 148, or even fewer. But at least some effort was being devoted to modernising what tanks were left in the West and in principle they continued to be accepted as an essential component of the ground forces.

List of books by the author on tanks and other armoured fighting vehicles

Armour: The Development of Armoured Forces and Their Equipment
(London, Stevens, 1960 and New York, Praeger, 1960)
Published in Italian as *I Corrazati* (Rome, Instituto per la Divulgazione
della Storia Militare, 1964 revised and published as *Armoured Forces*
(London, Arms and Armour Press, 1970)

Design and Development of Fighting Vehicles (London, Macdonald, 1968,
and New York, Doubleday, 1968) revised and published in Japanese as
Modern Fighting Vehicles (Tokyo, Gendai Kogakusha, 1986)

Technology of Tanks (2 vols) (Coulsdon, Jane's, 1991, revised and published
in German as *Technologie der Panzer* (Vienna, Verlag Herold, 1998)

Tanks: 100 Years of Evolution (Oxford, Osprey, 2015), second edition 2018
Published in Polish as *Czolgi: Sto Lat Historii* (Warsaw, Wydawnistwo RM,
2016), Published in Russian as *Tankii sto ljet istorii* (Moscow, Akuba Atticus,
and Sofia, Colibri, 2019)